Learn Decorative Machine Stitching

Maybe you just purchased a new sewing machine with hundreds (or thousands) of stitches, or you're taking a second look at a machine you have and wondering how all those stitches can be used.

After all, how many hemlines can you embellish with marching ducks? What are all those umpteen versions of the scallop stitch staring at you from the machine's display panel?

While many people sew perfectly well with only a straight and zigzag stitch, life is a little ho-hum if that's all you use.

Most of today's machines offer many more options to explore, and that's the purpose of this book.

You don't have to have children to use decorative stitches with reckless abandon, and, despite rumors to the contrary, you can even use them on things for boys and men. These fun stitches can be used for appliqué, quilting, hemming, couching, applying bias, embellishing piping, edge finishing and a host of other tasks, including stitching them out for just plain fun!

So, get out your machine manual, lurking somewhere "safe," and turn to the chapter that shows you what stitches you have and how to set the machine to use them. Let's get started.

Linda

Make Your Mark,
page 20

Meet the Designer

Linda is a lifelong sewer. Beginning at age 4, she made her first garment and by elementary school she started sewing things for friends, so it was destined that she have a career in the industry. She loves machine work, but handwork not so much!

Since receiving a degree in clothing and textiles from Oregon State University, she has taught high school, college and adult education classes. She has worked as a sewing machine company educator, a sewing product development manager for Harry & David, and as the editor of *Sew News* magazine. As owner of G Wiz Creative Services, she writes, edits and designs for a number of book and magazine publishers. She also leads fabric shopping tours to Hong Kong and other cities.

Linda currently lives in Bend, Ore., with her husband, Keith, a fabric store manager, and three dogs, Riley, Buckley and Frank, who love the idea that she works from home.

Table of Contents

11 Card Party

17 Whale of a Bib

20 Make Your Mark

24 Buttoned-Down Ornaments

28 Quilted Case

31 Going in Circles

34 Wrap It Up

38 Little Black Bag

43 Just Encase Gift-Card Holder

49 Crossing the Line

51 Soft Pocket Lingerie Keeper

54 It's a Wrap Gift Bag

57 Middle Management

60 Yipes, Stripes! Tote

General Instructions, 3
Sources, **64**
Photo Index, **64**

Going in Circles,
page 31

Yipes, Stripes! Tote,
page 60

*Just Encase
Gift-Card Holder,*
page 43

Basic Sewing Supplies & Equipment

- Sewing machine and matching thread
- Hand-sewing needles and thimble
- Straight pins and pincushion
- Seam ripper
- Removable fabric marking pens or tailor's chalk
- Measuring tools: tape measure and ruler
- Pattern tracing paper or cloth
- Point turner

- Pressing tools
- Pressing equipment: board and iron, and press cloths
- Rotary cutter, mats and straightedges
- Scissors
- Seam sealant
- Serger (optional)
- Fabric spray adhesive (optional)

General Instructions

Your sewing machine has two types of stitches—utility and decorative. Utility stitches have a sewing construction purpose, such as stitching a seam, overcasting an edge, hemming or mending. Decorative stitches, on the other hand, are just for fun and embellishing the things you sew.

However, these stitch categories are not mutually exclusive. A zigzag stitch that is stitched with standard sewing thread keeps a raw edge intact. The zigzag personae changes from mundane to marvelous when stitched with a specialty thread like metallic, variegated rayon or silk.

On the flip side, the decorative scallop stitch can be used to topstitch a hem in place—a very utilitarian use.

So, let's consider any stitch in your machine as one having decorative applications, no matter how it's listed in your machine manual.

Changing Appearances

There are many ways to change the appearance of a single stitch—making adjustments to the width and/or length, changing threads, adjusting tensions or combining it with other stitches.

Long & Narrow, Short & Wide

Most sewing machines allow you to change the stitch length and width to customize a stitch's appearance. However, a few machines offer only pre-set stitch length and width combinations. Check your manual or the machine to see which options you have and how to make length and width changes.

Changing the length of a stitch will alter its appearance by spreading out the stitches used to shape the design.

Altering the width of the stitch will affect its prominence.

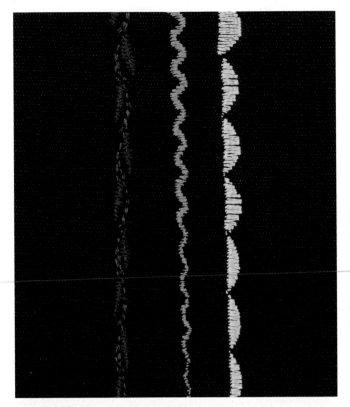

Other more complex stitches require that the machine sews both forward and backward to form the stitch. These stitches are referred to as reverse-cycle stitches and include ducks, Greek keys and smocking stitches. Much more thread is involved in the formation of these stitches, so adjustments may be required when using heavier weight threads.

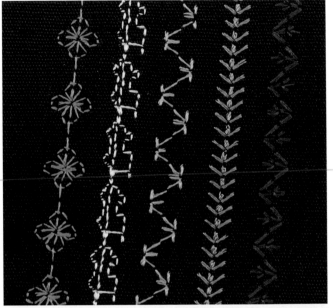

Forward & Backward

Some machine stitches are formed by a forward motion as the machine sews. Examples are straight stitching, zigzagging and scallops and waves.

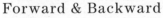

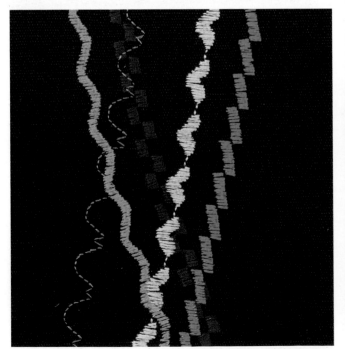

Some decorative motifs, like outlined flowers and vines, are openwork.

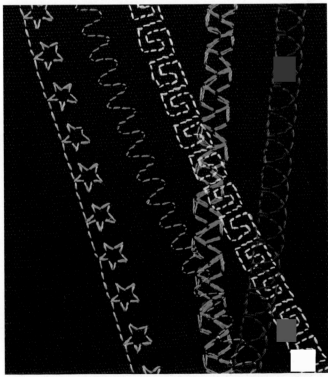

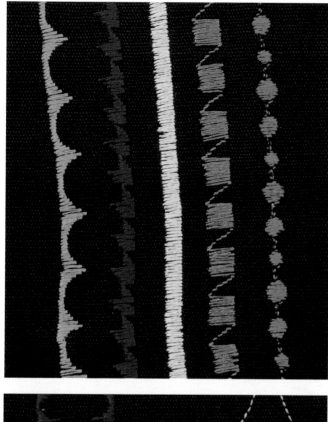

Some decorative motifs, like scallops and waves, are satin stitched, which creates a denser stitching. More stabilization may be needed for denser motifs, depending on the fabric used.

Opposites Attract

Many machines that offer decorative stitches also offer a function called mirror imaging. Mirror imagining will reverse the direction of a stitch from front to back and/or right to left, depending on the stitch.

With this option, ducks can be marching right to left or left to right, without changing the fabric direction as it goes through the machine. And scallop stitches can oppose each other in subsequent rows for edgings and trims.

Consult your owner's manual to see if your machine offers mirror imaging options and how to make the adjustment. Remember, side-to-side mirror imaging only affects stitches that are not symmetrical.

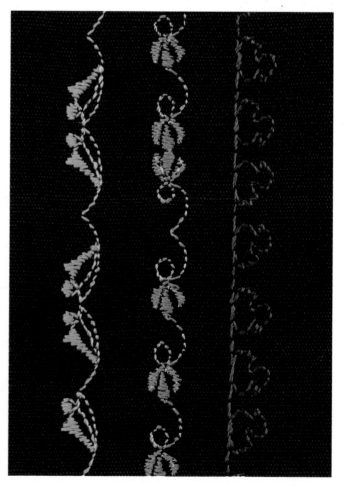

Thread Tactics

Most of us are used to conventional sewing threads made of polyester, cotton or cotton/polyester blends. They serve us well for constructing projects of all kinds. But, there is more to explore! Take a walk through your local fabric or quilt store, sewing machine dealership or online resource and you'll be amazed at all the thread types available.

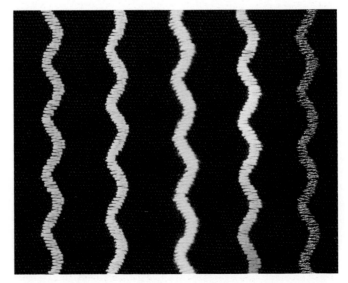

Threads, like people, come in different weights. Decorative threads come in a common range of 60-weight through 12-weight. In the world of thread, the bigger the weight number indicated, the finer the thread.

A 60-weight thread is very thin and often used in the bobbin or when stitching on very fine fabrics like voile and other sheers. It is common to find 60-weight threads in the same colors as heavier threads. Use the lightweight thread in the bobbin and matching thread in a heavier weight on the top of a project.

The larger the thread, the bigger the visual impact of the stitch you are sewing. For a bold statement, use a larger thread. For a more subtle appearance, choose a smaller size.

Some threads are even larger than size 12, but they can't be put through a needle. Instead, they can be used in the bobbin and stitching completed sewing upside down, with the wrong side of the fabric up as you stitch. (See Bobbin Work on page 10.)

Keep in mind the fabric weight when selecting thread weights. While a fine thread can be used on any fabric, the reverse isn't necessarily true. A large thread on a thin or fragile fabric can be a recipe for disaster.

In addition to weight, threads also differ in their fiber content and resulting appearance. Cotton, wool and acrylic threads create stitches with a matte finish; rayons, silks and metallics create stitches with shine. Polyester thread can appear either matte or shiny depending on the thread's construction and twist.

For added fun, there's glow-in-the-dark thread available in several colors. Once the thread has been exposed to light, it then glows for a short time. What child wouldn't love a secret message stitched on their pillowcase, or stars sprinkled on pajamas?

For outdoor aficionados, there's solar reactive thread. It is available in white or color, but when exposed to the sunlight, it turns a brighter shade of itself. How fun would this thread be for stitching flowers on bridesmaid dresses for a garden wedding? They're white and barely noticed indoors, and when the procession goes outside, they bloom in colors.

Thinking of thread as a single color strand? Think again. There are many kinds of variegated threads on the market today. Some offer gradual changes in color, others a more pronounced contrast along the strand. Variegated threads can produce stripes or more subtle color changes when stitched, depending on the thread's character. There's no way to know how the thread will showcase until you test-sew it with the stitch you're planning to use.

Make a sampler using the same stitch, but with different threads.

Needle Nuances

Closely related to thread choice is needle selection. The needle eye has to be large enough for the chosen thread to pass through it without abrasion as the stitches are formed. If the eye isn't large enough, shredding and breakage can occur.

Needles are sized using two numbers with a slash between, like 60/8. The first number is the metric sizing system and the second number is the American sizing system. The larger the number the bigger the needle shaft diameter and consequently the bigger hole it will make in the fabric. Household needles come in size 60/9 to 120/19. The size choice depends on the fabric weight and thread combination.

In addition to size options, there are also several types of needles designed for special uses. A universal needle is most commonly used for decorative stitching, but occasionally it's necessary to use a metallic needle with an elongated eye to coddle fragile metallic threads. On some fabrics, a Microtex or sharp needle penetrates the fabric surface easier, and on still other fabrics, like denim, a jeans needle pierces the dense weave. An embroidery needle has a slightly larger eye than others of the same size designation to allow decorative threads a smoother pass through fabrics without excess friction.

You can create interesting stitch patterning with double or triple needles. These multi-stitch parallel rows of the same stitch and you can use matching or contrasting threads to vary the effects even more. There is a width limitation when using multiple needles, and some machines even have a built-in warning system to alert you to the danger of potential needle breakage if you set the stitch too wide. The multiple needles can easily go crashing into the needle plate and break. Check your machine manual for the proper settings when using multiple needles for decorative stitching.

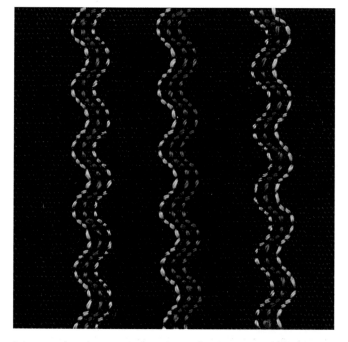

It's good to have a selection of various needle sizes and types on hand for test stitching; if your machine balks at one type, you can try another without a shopping adventure.

Tension Headaches

One of the things sewers fear most is tension. Perhaps from a young age you've been warned not to touch the machine's tension. Many of today's machines don't require much tension adjustment for normal sewing, but when you venture outside of "normal" into the world of decorative threads and stitches, it's helpful to understand tension.

Tension is quite simply the amount of pull on the thread as it forms a stitch. There is upper tension, created by discs that clamp down on the threads as they go through the machine threading path. Upper thread tension can be digital, or adjusted by a dial. A higher number indicates more pull on the thread, and a lower number, a lesser pull.

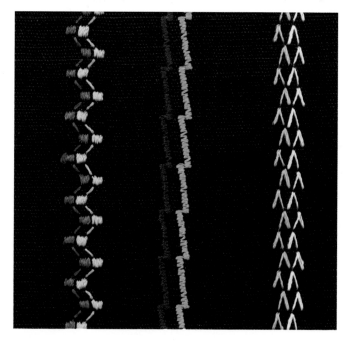

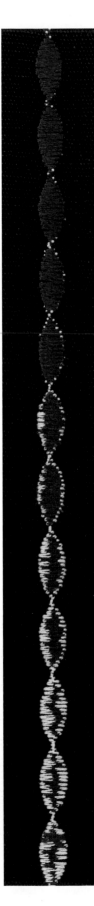

There is also lower tension that exerts pull as the thread comes out of the bobbin. If your machine has a bobbin case, there will be a tiny screw on the side of the case. If it's a drop-in bobbin, there will be a screw on the bobbin housing. Neither is numbered as the top tension adjustment mechanism is.

Thread tension needs to be balanced for a perfect stitch. Think of tension as a tug-of-war—the two forces (upper and lower) need to be equal so that the bobbin and top thread meet in the middle of the fabric thickness. The bobbin thread shouldn't show on the top side, and the needle thread shouldn't show on the bottom side.

When you're using decorative stitches and novelty threads, it may be necessary to adjust the tensions to keep the stitches looking perfect. If you use one weight of thread in the needle and another in the bobbin, an unbalanced stitch can easily occur.

If the upper thread shows on the bobbin side, tighten the upper tension. If the bobbin thread shows on the top side, loosen the upper tension. Since the upper thread tension adjustment is numbered, it's easier to adjust it than the bobbin tension screw, so start there to rebalance the stitch.

If your stitching puckers the fabric, try loosening the upper tension slightly to flatten it. But your fabric may also need some stabilization to support the thread bulk.

Stabilizer Smarts
Not all fabric weights can support decorative stitching and still remain flat. As thread is pounded into a relatively small area, it can cause fabric to pucker and no amount of pressing will flatten the stitches. Using a very wide, dense stitch may also cause the fabric to "tunnel," pulling the left and right edges toward the middle creating a visible dip in the center of the stitch. Tunneling won't press out either.

The answer to getting stitched fabric to lie flat can be stabilizing it before stitching. Adding a stabilizer behind the stitching area gives the area more body to be able to support the thread-dense stitching.

There are several kinds of stabilizers available. Some stay with the project permanently and are cut away close to the stitching after it's completed. Others stabilize only temporarily during the stitching process, and then they're removed when the stitching is complete. Stabilizer may be simply laid under the fabric for stitching, or it may be adhered to it either by fusing with an iron or with self-adhesion. Still another type of stabilizer is liquid and is actually brushed into the fabric and allowed to dry prior to stitching; once the stitching is complete, it's washed away.

In lieu of stabilizer, some fabrics may be starched or sprayed with a starch alternative or sizing to stiffen them for stitching. That finish then washes out later.

As you work through the projects in this book, you'll use different types of stabilizers to improve stitch quality.

Tip
It's a good idea to test-sew every decorative stitch before you actually use it on your project. Not only do you get to see how the thread stitches out, but also you can make any needle, length, width or tension adjustments needed for picture-perfect stitching.

Foot Notes
Decorative stitching can build up lots of thread in a small area and it's important that the machine's presser foot allows that bulk to pass under it without obstruction. If not, stitches can become distorted and uneven.

Your machine may have a clear plastic or a metal foot especially designed for use with decorative stitching. It's usually called a satin stitch foot and has an indentation on the underside to allow bulky stitch build-up to slide right under. Check your manual to see which foot is recommended for your machine.

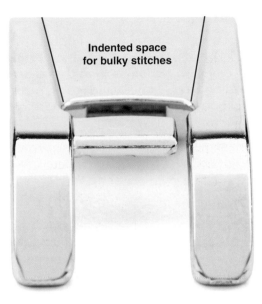

Indented space for bulky stitches

Stitching Straight

Keeping rows of decorative stitching straight can be done in several ways:

Use a removable marker to draw lines on the fabric.

Guide the presser foot along a fabric edge if you're stitching near one, like for hemming.

Follow a recognizable part of the fabric patterning, like stitching along a stripe, plaid or border design printed or woven into the fabric.

Use a quilting guide attachment to evenly space the stitching line from a drawn line, previously stitched row, or from a fabric edge or seam.

And what if you don't want stitches in a straight line but prefer a free-form patterning? Use a removable marker and draw lines as you wish—or not. Same goes for circles. Decorative stitches can go in any shape, but note that it's easier to guide the forward-motion stitches into tight spaces than it is to guide reverse-cycle stitches because of the backward/forward motion needed to shape the patterning.

Don't forget—stitches can also cross each other or be placed side by side to create other pattern variations.

In the End

It's ideal if rows of decorative stitching can begin and end in a seam line, but that's not always the case. If the decorative line will be crossed by another row of stitching of any kind, it's not necessary to anchor the thread ends. But if that isn't the case, some protection is needed to keep threads from unraveling.

One option is to leave threads long at the beginning and end of the stitched row. Pull the threads to the underside and tie in a secure knot; clip threads close to the knot.

Another option is to apply a fray stopper liquid to the ends of the stitching to secure it. When the liquid is thoroughly dry, clip off the thread ends close to the stitching.

Some machines have a "fix" or "lock" function which allows it to stitch in one place to anchor threads at the beginning and/or end of a row of stitching. If your machine has this function, use it and clip threads close to the stitching.

Program Mode

Machine capabilities vary greatly, but many machines offer the option of programming decorative stitches into the memory. This allows you to create customized sequences of different motifs and store them for use at another time. It provides more variety than simply stitching out the same stitch repeatedly in a line. For example, you can program in flowers and leaves together.

Most machines also have a way that you can stitch out a single motif. For example, if you only want one flower, not a line of

them, pushing the single motif button tells the machine to stop stitching after one pattern.

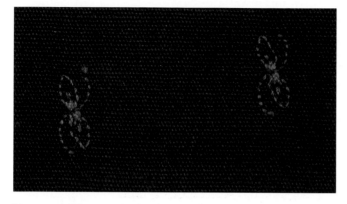

Your machine may also have a button to designate "pattern start." If you engage this function, the machine will begin stitching at the starting point of a given pattern (like a scallop) instead of starting half way through the design, which may be where you stopped stitching with the previous one. This function is especially helpful if you're trying to match up the design patterning for trims and edges.

Bobbin Work

When you want to use threads that are too big to fit through the eye of the needle, use them in the bobbin instead and sew your designs upside down! Threads like twisted floss, rayon and silk ribbon, woolies and other cords can be hand-wound onto the machine bobbin.

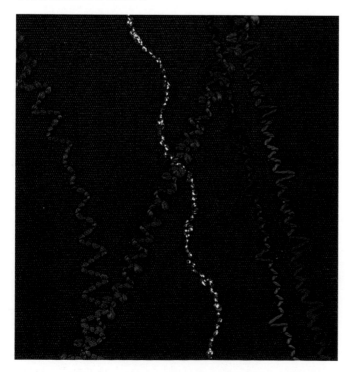

Regular sewing thread is used on the top side of the machine to coordinate or contrast with the bobbin thread, depending on the look you like. Since you're hand-winding, try not to stretch any flexible threads as you wind, and spread them evenly across the bobbin height as you wind.

If your machine has a removable bobbin case, most often you'll need to bypass the tension spring with the heavier thread, simply leaving that area out of the threading path. Some brands of machines have accessory bobbin cases you can purchase designed specifically for bobbin work.

If your machine has a drop-in bobbin, bypass the tension slot with the heavier threads.

Some bobbin cases have a hole in the extended point, through which heavier threads can be threaded to give them a bit of tension.

It's a matter of experimentation for the lower threading process, as each machine differs in how it responds to the heavier threads. So pick a thread, pick a stitch and play with it to get a look you like.

Tip

When using heavy threads in the bobbin, you don't have much thread length to stitch with, so pick a project with a short length to embellish, or carefully tie threads at the joining on the fabric wrong side. The belt on page 57 is ideal for bobbin work, as stitching distances are short.

Because you're sewing upside down, it's easy to mark stitching lines on the wrong side. Using a stabilizer under the stitching (on top as you're sewing) creates the perfect canvas for drawing your lines, and it helps to keep the stitching from puckering with the heavier threads.

At the end of your stitching line, if it's not in a seam, leave 3-inch-long thread tails to pull to the fabric wrong side and tie off. ■

Card Party

Using die-cut card blanks with fabric inserts is a great way to try out all kinds of decorative machine stitches. A trip through the paper-crafting department of your favorite craft store will add pizzazz to your stitching with accents of all kinds. Warning: Card making is addictive!

Finished Size
4 x 6 inches

Materials
See materials lists for individual cards for specific materials.

- Die-cut trifold card blanks*
- Assorted fabric scraps (at least 4 x 6 inches)

- 30-weight rayon machine embroidery threads*
- Lightweight cotton batting*
- Double-sided scrapbooking tape
- Fabric glue*
- Repositionable tape
- Embellishments
- Assorted ribbon, trim, floss, buttons
- Glitter, embossed and dimensional paper-crafting stickers
- Embossed sentiment stickers
- Basic sewing supplies and equipment

*Paper Creations Quilt-a-Card™; Sulky® 30-weight rayon machine embroidery threads; Warm & White® batting from The Warm Company; Beacon Adhesives™ Fabri-Tac™ glue used to make samples.

Card Blanks

Trifold die-cut card blanks work best with embellished fabrics. One of the three sections folds over and covers the back of the embellished fabric for a professional-looking finish. These card blanks are available with openings of assorted shapes for many occasions.

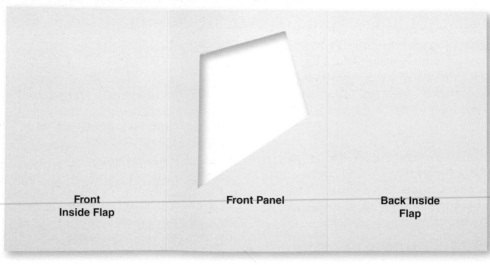

Front
Inside Flap

Front Panel

Back Inside
Flap

General Assembly

1. Choose a background fabric from the assorted fabric scraps. Cut a 4 x 6-inch rectangle each from the background fabric and batting.

2. Layer background fabric on the batting and stitch lines of assorted decorative stitches equal distances apart; press.

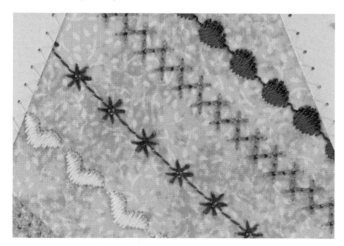

3. Set the machine for a medium-width and medium-length zigzag stitch.

4. Punch out the die-cut opening in the card blank. Place the stitched fabric piece right side down on the front panel. Secure in place with repositionable tape.

5. Turn card over and stitch around the die-cut opening edges using the zigzag stitch. *Note: If your card will have an embellishment like a kite tail, begin and end stitching where the embellishment will be placed.*

6. End the stitching exactly at the starting point, leaving long thread ends. Pull the thread ends to the back and tie off.

7. Trim the stitched fabric piece just outside the stitching line.

8. Position double-sided tape along the edges of the front inside flap referring to Card Blanks.

9. Fold the front inside flap over the front panel and finger-press to secure over the front panel.

10. Add embellishments as desired to complement the card front.

Birthday Party Invitation

Materials
- Bright color fabric scrap (at least 4 x 6 inches)
- Coordinating machine embroidery thread
- 3 (¼ yard) pieces of ¼-inch-wide ribbon to coordinate with thread and background fabric
- Glitter stickers: alphabet, assorted stars
- 1-inch flat-back flower button

Assembly
1. Prepare the background fabric/batting following steps 1 and 2 of the General Assembly instructions. Use the presser foot edge for spacing and stitch diagonal rows of decorative stitches across the background fabric/batting referring again to step 2.

2. Follow General Assembly steps 3–9. In step 5, begin and end stitching at the hat point.

3. To embellish the birthday hat, apply glitter alphabet stickers to the bottom right-hand corner of the card front, spelling "party." Add glitter stars around hat.

4. Tie the three ribbons together at the center. Glue the knot to the hat point.

5. Position and glue the 1-inch flat-back button over the ribbon knot. Trim the ribbon ends if necessary.

Love Card

Materials
- 7 coordinating fabric scraps
- Coordinating machine embroidery threads
- ⅝ yard rosebud trim
- Dimensional sentiment stickers

Assembly
1. Cut seven 1 x 6-inch strips from assorted coordinating fabric scraps.

2. Choose and position one fabric strip right side up on the left edge of a 4 x 6-inch batting piece (Figure 1a).

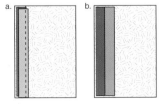

Figure 1

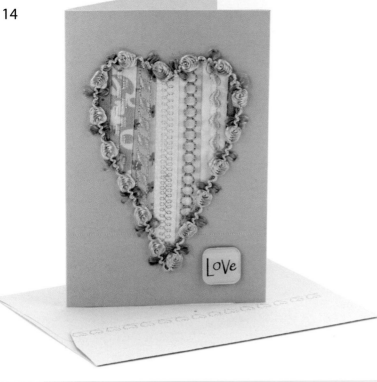

3. Position a second strip right side down, matching raw edges with first strip. Stitch strips together along right edge using a ¼-inch seam referring again to Figure 1a. Finger-press the second strip to the right (Figure 1b).

4. Continue in the same manner until the batting rectangle is covered.

5. Decoratively stitch down each strip center.

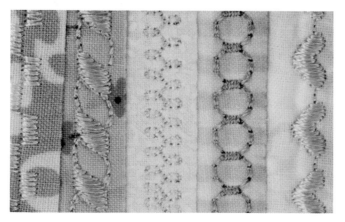

Send Off

If you embellish the cards with anything thicker than ¼ inch (like pompoms, shank buttons, etc.), you will need to use a padded envelope to send the card to the recipient. Check with the post office for details and restrictions.

6. Follow General Assembly steps 3–9 to complete construction.

7. Glue rose bud trim over the cutout edge, meeting ends at top center of heart; trim excess.

8. Add a dimensional sentiment sticker to lower right of the card front panel.

Kite

Materials
- Coordinating solid and narrow stripe fabric scraps
- Coordinating machine embroidery threads
- 3 (8-inch) pieces coordinating embroidery floss
- 4 (4-inch) pieces ⅛-inch-wide satin ribbon
- Embossed sentiment stickers

Assembly
1. Cut two 2¼ x 4-inch pieces each from solid and narrow stripe fabrics. Alternating the stripes' directions as shown in Figure 2a, stitch a stripe piece to a solid along the long edges. Press seams in opposite directions.

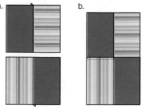

Figure 2

2. Join the pieces together matching seams referring to Figure 2b. Press seam in one direction.

3. Layer the fabric over the batting referring to step 2 of General Assembly. Embellish the solid fabric sections with decorative stitches. Stitch a decorative stitch over the seams.

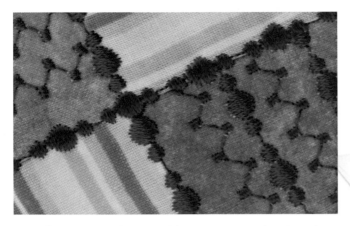

4. Follow General Assembly steps 3–9, aligning the seams with the kite points on the card cutout.

5. Knot the ends of the embroidery floss pieces together. Lightly glue ends in place at bottom of kite and on bottom right side of front panel to form the kite tail; trim excess length if needed.

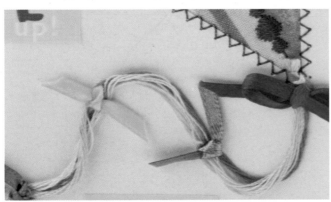

6. Make small bows and ties from the ⅛-inch satin ribbon and glue in place along the kite tail length.

7. Add embossed sentiment stickers to the card front panel referring to the sample photo. ■

The Envelope, Please

Surprise the recipient (and the post office) with a stitched envelope flap.

Use a design to coordinate with the card, but choose stitches that are not too dense, or the paper will simply perforate and tear.

To anchor the thread ends, bring them to the back and tie a small knot, or trim and apply seam sealant to prevent raveling.

Whale of a Bib

There is something adorable about babies, but when they're dressed in cute and practical things, they're even more appealing. Use your machine's decorative stitches for appliqué and edge finishing.

Finished Size
7½ x 8½ inches

Materials
- ⅓ yard stripe
- ⅓ yard print
- ⅓ yard woven fusible interfacing
- 6-inch-square fabric scrap
- 1¾ yards double-fold bias tape
- Paper-back fusible web*
- Tear-away fabric stabilizer*
- Temporary spray adhesive*
- 30-weight rayon machine embroidery thread*
- Matching threads for bobbin*
- Basic sewing supplies and equipment

*The Warm Company Steam-A-Seam 2® paper-back fusible web; Sulky® 30-weight rayon machine embroidery thread, KK2000™ Temporary Spray Adhesive and Tear-Easy™ stabilizer used to make sample.

Cutting
Use pattern templates for Bib and Whale appliqué on page 19. Transfer all pattern markings to fabric.

From the stripe fabric:
- Fold stripe fabric with stripes running vertically. Cut one bib on fold using pattern provided.
- Cut one 3 x 9-inch bib pocket rectangle with stripes running horizontally.

From the print fabric:
- Cut one bib for lining on fold using pattern provided.

From the fusible interfacing:
- Cut one bib on fold using pattern provided.
- Cut one 6-inch square.
- Cut one 3 x 9-inch rectangle for bib pocket.

Stitching the Appliqué
1. Fuse the fusible interfacing bib and 6-inch square to the wrong sides of the fabric scrap and striped bib.

2. Trace one whale shape onto the paper side of the fusible web. Cut out whale leaving ¼-inch margin around shape.

3. Follow the manufacturer's instructions and fuse the fusible web shape to the wrong side of the fabric scrap. Cut out the whale along the drawn lines and remove paper backing.

4. Position the whale centered and 2 inches up from the bib lower edge referring to Figure 1. Fuse in place following the manufacturer's instructions.

Figure 1

5. Spray a 6-inch square of tear-away stabilizer with temporary spray adhesive and position on wrong side of bib behind appliqué area.

6. Set your sewing machine for an appliqué stitch and stitch around the whale edges. *Note: The stitch should span the whale and the bib fabric for a secure hold. To keep the stitch perpendicular to the fabric edge, stop and pivot occasionally.*

7. Set your sewing machine to sew a small eyelet. Position and stitch the eyelet over the whale's eye indicated on the appliqué pattern.

8. Set your sewing machine for a narrow satin stitch and stitch the whale's smile following the line indicated on the appliqué pattern.

9. Set your sewing machine for a bubble stitch and stitch three lines for the whale's spout, curving the stitching to keep the lines free of the neckline seam allowance.

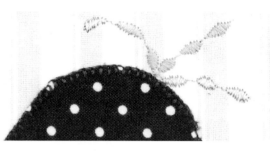

10. Carefully tear away the stabilizer after stitching is completed.

On the Edge

Trimming fabric close to a decorative edge stitching, like the wave lines on the bib pocket edge, can be a challenge. You want to trim the excess fabric without cutting any stitches. But, you also don't want to leave scraggly edges.

Carefully trim as close as you can to the stitching using small sharp scissors. Hide any errant fabric threads by coloring the trimmed edge using a permanent marker that matches the thread color. Permanent markers come in hundreds of colors. **Note:** This technique works only if the thread color is darker than the background fabric.

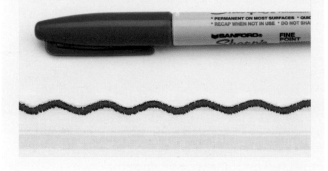

Completing the Whale Bib

1. Fuse the interfacing to the wrong side of the pocket rectangle.

2. Set your sewing machine for a dense wave stitch. Stitch ½-inch from the upper pocket rectangle edge.

3. Closely trim the fabric away from the stitching using small sharp scissors and referring to On the Edge for tips.

4. Stitch two more short rows of waves near the bib pocket center approximately ½ inch apart.

5. Mark the center of the bib pocket. Position and pin the bib pocket over the bib, overlapping the whale appliqué lower edge approximately ¼ inch.

6. Turn the bib/pocket bib side up and baste the layers together close to the bib outer edges. Trim the pocket to match the bib shape (Figure 2).

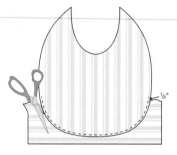

Figure 2

7. Spray the print bib lining wrong side with temporary spray adhesive and position wrong sides together with the bib, matching all the edges. Smooth the layers together.

8. Apply bias tape to the bib outer edges using a medium width and length zigzag stitch (Figure 3).

Figure 3

9. Cut a 30-inch length of bias tape for the neck opening/ties and pin-mark the center.

10. Bind the bib neckline matching the bias and neckline centers. ***Note:** Begin stitching the bias tie portion, then the bib section and the remaining half of the tie. If your machine has difficulty stitching on bias tape with no fabric under it, hold the bias gently front and back to help with even feeding or place tear-away fabric stabilizer under the tie sections.*

11. Knot the tie ends and trim diagonally.

12. Hand-embroider fish shapes, below, to the pocket section only referring to the project photo. ∎

Stitch Smart

This project uses the following decorative stitches: appliqué, eyelet, wave, bubbles and satin. If your machine doesn't have the same stitches, choose something close for a similar look.

Whale of a Bib
Whale Bib
Cut 1 on fold from stripe fabric
Cut 1 on fold from print fabric
Cut 1 on fold from fusible interfacing

Place on fold

Pocket Placement

Whale of a Bib
Whale Appliqué
Cut per instructions

Whale of a Bib
Fish
Cut per instructions

Make Your Mark

Bookmarks are a great way to use a variety of machine stitches. Sewing on felt is easy for beginners and even children can sew their favorite stitches on these quick gifts.

Finished Size
Approximately 2½ x 9 inches or size desired

Bookmark Sizes

Bookmarks can be any size you want them to be. Some common sizes are 2 x 6, 2 x 8, 2 x 10 and 3 x 7 inches. To display your decorative stitches, bigger is better of course.

Materials

- ⅛ yard each or 1 (9 x 12-inch) piece each, color desired:
    Wool or synthetic bookmark felt
    Wool or synthetic backing felt
- Assorted machine embroidery threads*:
    12-weight cotton
    30-weight rayon
    Matching bobbin threads
- Paper-back fusible web*
- Tear-away stabilizer*
- Temporary spray adhesive*
- Chalk marker
- Assorted embellishments:
    yarns
    buttons
    charms
    ribbons
    beads
- Seam sealant*
- Novelty edge scissors or rotary cutting blades (optional)
- Basic sewing supplies and equipment

*The Warm Company Steam-A-Seam 2® paper-back fusible web; Sulky® 30-weight rayon machine embroidery thread and 12-weight cotton Blendables®, KK2000™ Temporary Spray Adhesive and Tear-Easy™ stabilizer; June Tailor Fray Block™ used to make samples.

Felt Tips

Felt yardage is usually wide—up to 72 inches! You can get many bookmarks from the required yardage. If you don't want that many bookmarks, purchase 9 x 12-inch felt pieces.

Use contrast-colored felt as a backing accent to cover the underside of the stitching.

If using synthetic felt, be sure to use a pressing cloth when applying fusible web.

Cutting

From bookmark and backing felt:
- Cut one strip each 3 x 10 inches or the size desired for each bookmark.

From tear-away stabilizer:
- Cut one 3½ x 10½-inch strip or a strip slightly larger than the felt.

General Assembly

1. Spray the stabilizer strip with temporary adhesive and apply to the wrong side of the bookmark felt strip.

2. Draw a chalk line down the lengthwise center of the strip to use as a stitching guide (Figure 1).

Figure 1

3. Stabilize scrap strips of felt in the same manner for stitching test strips.

4. Select the stitches you prefer and test-stitch on a scrap of stabilized felt. Adjust the tension, length and width to the desired look referring to the General Instructions on page 3.

5. Stitch as desired referring to Decorating Options on page 22.

6. Before trimming the stitched felt, place a line of seam sealant along the beginning and end of stitching to prevent threads from raveling. Let the seam sealant dry thoroughly.

7. Trim the stitched felt strip to 2 x 9 inches or the size desired. **Note:** *Use novelty-edge scissors or rotary cutting blades to give the edges interest.*

8. Gently tear away the stabilizer from the edges of the stitched felt.

9. Follow the manufacturer's instructions to apply paper-backed fusible web to the wrong side of the stitched felt strip and remove the paper backing.

10. Select any yarn, thread or ribbon trim and cut several 10-inch or desired length pieces.

11. Center the stitched felt on the backing felt and place trim ends between the two layers at one short end (Figure 2).

Figure 2

12. Fuse layers together, following fusible web manufacturer's instructions. *Note: Synthetic felt may require a press cloth.*

13. Trim the felt backing edges leaving a contrast color border. *Note: Use novelty-edge scissors or rotary cutting blades to give the edges interest.*

14. Secure any buttons, beads or charms to the ends of the yarn, ribbon or thread pieces.

Decorating Options

Straight Rows of Decorative Stitches

Choose a variety of decorative stitches to fill the bookmark with rows spaced equally apart across the bookmark width.

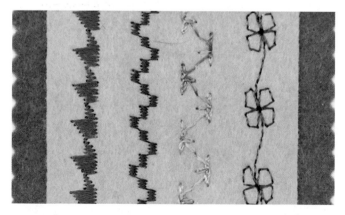

1. Cut and prepare bookmark felt and test desired stitches referring to cutting instructions and steps 1–4 of General Assembly.

2. Stitch down the center of the bookmark felt on or beside the drawn line with first decorative stitch.

3. Position the presser foot next to the center row of stitching for spacing and continue stitching subsequent rows from the center outward.

4. Complete the bookmark following steps 6–14 of General Assembly.

Couched Strands

Using decorative machine stitches to couch or sew over strands of yarn, cord or ribbon trim adds interest and a new look to the stitches.

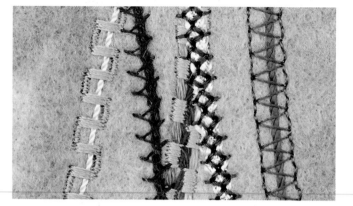

1. Cut and prepare bookmark felt and test desired stitches referring to cutting instructions and steps 1–3 of General Assembly.

2. Select yarn, cord or ribbon trim to stitch over and cut 8–10 inches longer than the bookmark felt.

3. Select and attach a buttonhole, cording or multiple-hole foot for your machine. These feet provide room for the strands of yarn, cord or ribbon trim you have chosen to use to slide underneath the presser foot.

Holey Foot, Man!

Some machine brands offer an optional presser foot with multiple holes in the front to help guide strands of yarn, ribbon or heavy threads for couching.

One or more strands go through each hole, and the spacing is such that the widest stitch

width will encase all the threads.

Check with your dealer to see if one is available for your machine model.

4. Choose a decorative stitch wide enough to encase the trims you have chosen to use, but open enough to let them show through the stitching.

5. Use the stabilized felt scrap strips to test your stitch choices. Begin by leaving about 3 inches of trim at the upper end of the test strip.

6. Stitch the design, guiding the trim under the foot to keep it centered and encased by the stitching. Adjust the tension, length and width to the desired look referring to the General Instructions on page 3.

7. After testing all stitch choices, stitch the prepared bookmark felt as desired. *Note: Stitched lines don't have to be in vertical rows—they can meander and cross each other if desired. Be aware that some machines may distort the pattern stitching slightly when crossing over thick areas.*

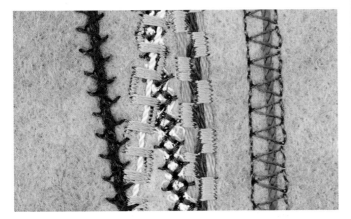

8. At the lower end of the felt strip, leave 4 inches of each trim. Tie off the stitch threads on the underside of the felt.

9. Follow steps 8–14 of General Assembly to complete the bookmark.

Programmed Stitches
Some machines with decorative stitches have a memory function to allow for programming stitch combinations and alphabet letters.

You can spell words, combine different stitches in varying repeat patterns and combine letters with stitches. This allows you to add a name to the bookmark, and have some stitch variety.

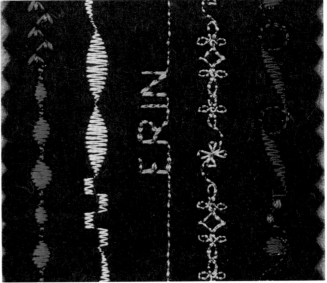

1. Consult your machine manual for information on programming designs.

2. Cut and prepare bookmark felt referring to cutting instructions and steps 1–3 of General Assembly.

3. Test desired stitches referring to step 4 of General Assembly and your machine manual.

4. Stitch as desired and complete the bookmark following General Assembly steps 6–14. ■

Buttoned-Down Ornaments

Cover-your-own-button forms help create these fun ornaments. They are available up to 2½ inches in diameter and simply snap together for holiday decorating fun.

Finished Size
2½-inch diameter

Materials
Materials listed make one ornament.

- 4-inch square background fabric
- 12-inch length narrow trim, piping or rickrack
- 7-inch length ⅛-inch-wide double-faced satin ribbon
- 4-inch square felt
- 2½-inch diameter button covering kit*
- Fabric glue*
- Tear-away stabilizer*
- Temporary spray adhesive*
- 30-weight rayon, machine embroidery thread*
- Twin needle (optional)
- Basic sewing supplies and equipment

*Dritz™ Half Ball Cover Button; Sulky® 30-weight rayon machine embroidery thread, Tear-Easy™ stabilizer and KK2000™ Temporary Spray Adhesive; Beacon Adhesives™ Fabri-Tac™ glue used to make samples.

General Assembly
1. Spray the tear-away stabilizer with temporary adhesive and adhere to wrong side of 4-inch square of background fabric.

2. Embellish the fabric square with the stitches of your choice referring to Decorating Options on page 26.

3. Trace the circle template provided with the button kit onto the wrong side of the embellished fabric, centering the stitched design if desired.

4. Cut out the circle. Remove as much stabilizer as possible, especially around the edges for easier button covering.

5. Remove the button wire shank.

6. Lightly spray the domed portion of the button and adhere the stitched circle, centering the button form.

7. Working from opposite sides, pull the stitched fabric over the prongs on the underside of the button form. *Note: Ease in fabric with your fingernails, trying not to let tiny pleats form around the edge.*

8. Fold the ribbon in half and tape on the underside at the button upper edge center.

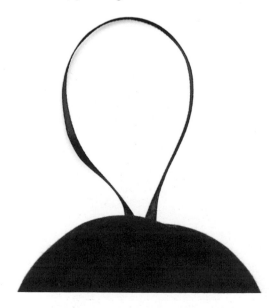

9. Snap the button back into the covered button. *Note: If the fabric is heavily embellished or thick, use a spool to help push the backing onto the button.*

10. Carefully glue any desired trim around the button perimeter beginning and ending behind the hanger ribbon.

11. Cut a 2¼-inch felt circle and glue in place over the button ornament back.

Tip

When covering a button form with a thin or light color fabric, add a layer of fusible interfacing to the fabric wrong side before stitching. This helps keep the metal form from showing through the finished ornament front.

If you prefer a puffier look, add a layer of batting between the button form and the stitched piece.

Decorating Options

Twin Needle Fun
Two needles, one shank—that's how it works.

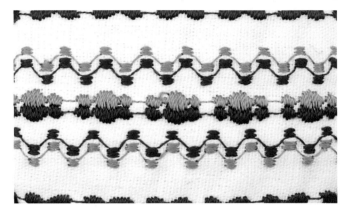

1. Check your machine manual for settings needed to use a double needle. On most machines, the stitch width is limited to keep the needles from running into the presser foot and needle hole. Some machines do this automatically; others require manual adjustment of the stitch width.

2. Double needles come in a variety of sizes and spacing. When you purchase a double needle, there are two numeric indications, such as 2.0/80. The first is the spacing in millimeters between the needles, and the second is the size of the needles.

Even though you have two needles in the machine, the one bobbin thread catches them both during the stitch formation process.

3. Most machines offer two spool pins to hold threads for double-needle work. Follow the instructions in your owner's manual for the threading pattern, as some machines separate threads at the tension disks and thread guides, and others won't.

4. Some adjustment to the stitch length may be necessary since you have twice as much thread in the same stitching space.

5. Test-stitch before working on your project to be sure needles clear the foot and needle plate opening.

6. Use the presser foot edge as a guide for spacing stitches after stitching the initial row.

Checkmate

This ornament is a fun use for checked fabric—the lines of the print serve as a guide for the stitching rows between.

1. Center the design lines under the presser foot and sew as many rows of stitches as you want to fill up the space.

2. Test-stitch before working on your project to be sure the stitch width fits within the printed lines on the fabric; adjust as needed.

3. Embellish this ornament with two felt holly leaves and three ¼-inch red pompom berries glued near the hanger referring to the photo.

Single Motifs

Most machines have a setting to allow you to stitch just a single motif. It is easy to fill up the button covering fabric square with single repeated designs, or mix and match with others for interest.

1. Stitch the motifs randomly or mark small dots where you want the motifs using a removable marker.

2. At the beginning and end of the pattern, the machine anchors the thread ends so you can pull them to the back and trim.

3. Then move to the next location and repeat the stitched motif.

4. Repeat to sew as many as you want. ■

Button, Button

The cover-your-own-button forms consist of two parts—the upper portion and the snap-on back.

When making ornaments, remove the snap-out wire shank and discard.

Quilted Case

There's nothing more comfy than a flannel shirt, and your e-reader or tablet deserves that same cozy care as well. This quilted case lets you transport it anywhere in style and the decorative stitch used for the quilting process highlights the fabric patterning. A handy inside pocket is perfect for the charger, instruction book or a tiny reading light.

Finished Size
10 x 7½ inches

Materials
• ¾ yard bias-plaid flannel
• ¾ yard solid flannel
• ¾ yard lightweight cotton batting*
• 18-inch zipper
• 2⅝ yards purchased coordinating piping
• 2⅝ yards single-fold bias tape
• 30-weight rayon, machine embroidery thread*
• Pattern tracing cloth
• Temporary spray adhesive*
• Walking or even-feed foot (optional)
• Basic sewing supplies and equipment
*The Warm Company Warm & Natural® batting; Sulky® 30-weight rayon machine embroidery thread and KK2000™ Temporary Spray Adhesive used to make sample.

Sizing for Your Device
E-readers and tablets come in many sizes. Instructions follow for drafting a pattern for your device. The yardage and items listed here will make a case that fits a reader about 10 x 7½ inches.

If your device is smaller, you may have leftover materials or you can purchase materials based on the pattern you have drafted to fit your device.

Cases can be made with a horizontal or vertical orientation, decide which orientation you prefer and draft your pattern accordingly.

Pattern Drafting
1. Measure your device and add 2¾ inches to the measured length and width. Cut a rectangle from pattern tracing cloth this size.

2. Fold the rectangle into fourths, aligning the corners. Measure and mark 2 inches out from the corner in each direction (Figure 1a).

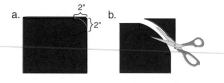

Figure 1

3. Create rounded corners by trimming between the marks using a plate or glass (Figure 1b).

4. To make the pocket pattern, determine the desired height of the pocket and double it. Cut a rectangle from pattern tracing cloth that size and round the corners using the case pattern.

Cutting
From the plaid flannel:
• Cut two rectangles 2 inches larger than the case pattern for case front and back.
• Cut one 1½ inches by width of fabric strip for side gusset.

From the solid flannel:
• Cut two rectangles 2 inches larger than the case pattern for case front and back.
• Cut one pocket pattern.
• Cut one 1½ inches by width of fabric strip for side gusset.

From cotton batting:
• Cut two rectangles 2 inches larger than the case pattern for case front and back.

Quilting & Decorative Stitching
1. Select a prominent line in the plaid and a decorative stitch that you like to accent the plaid pattern.

Learn Decorative Machine Stitching

2. Layer lining wrong side up, and cotton batting and plaid flannel right side up; spray-baste layers together smoothing into place. Repeat for the opposite case side.

3. Test-stitch your designs on small squares of layered fabric, batting and backing scraps.

4. When satisfied with the look of the stitch, quilt the layered case front and back on the plaid lines in one or both directions. *Note: Some stitches are directional, so stitch from top to bottom on all rows if you select one of these.*

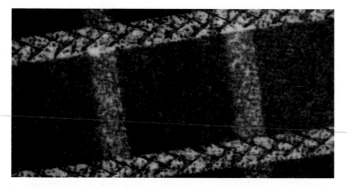

5. After the quilting is complete on both case front and back rectangles, trim the pieces using the case pattern you drafted.

Assembly

1. Fold the pocket in half and press.

2. Position and pin the pocket on the lining side of the case back, matching the lower corners (Figure 2). Baste in place.

Figure 2

3. Baste the piping around the case front and back edges using a zipper foot. Clip corner curves as needed (Figure 3). Overlap the piping ends into the seam allowance as shown in Figure 4.

Figure 3   **Figure 4**

4. Spray-baste the two gusset layers wrong sides together. Stitch plaid side of one gusset short end to the right side of zipper tab end.

5. Finger-press the gusset away from zipper. Topstitch once or twice across gusset to secure (Figure 5).

Figure 5

6. Determine how wide the case opening should be to easily get your reader in and out. Center the zipper across the determined case opening; shorten zipper length if necessary.

7. Pin-mark the zipper center and the opening center on the case front and back upper edges.

8. With the zipper partially open and right sides together, pin the zipper/gusset around the case matching the zipper center to the case front opening center (Figure 6).

Figure 6

9. If needed, trim the end of the gusset that is hanging free, allowing 1 inch of extra length for covering the zipper end referring again to Figure 6.

10. Stitch the zipper/gusset to the case, just inside the piping basting line. At the zipper end, fold the extra gusset length back and place under the zipper end. Continue stitching zipper/gusset to case.

11. Stitch case back to zipper/gusset/case front referring to steps 7–10 and Figure 7.

Figure 7

12. Finish interior of case by binding the inside seam allowances with purchased binding or finishing with zigzag, overedge stitches or a serger. ∎

Going in Circles

Round and round we go! Showcasing your machine's decorative stitches with circular sewing creates a whole new dimension. Sew full circles, arcs or a combination of both to show off your favorite stitches.

Finished Size
14 x 42 inches

Materials
- ½ yard batik print
- ½ yard print
- ½ yard lightweight cotton batting*
- 2 (4-inch) tassels
- Tear-away fabric stabilizer*
- Self-adhesive fabric stabilizer*
- Temporary spray fabric adhesive*
- Variety 12-weight cotton, machine embroidery thread*
- Variety 30-weight rayon, machine embroidery thread*
- Basic sewing supplies and equipment

The Warm Company Warm & White® batting; Sulky® 12-weight cotton Blendables® and 30-weight rayon machine embroidery threads, KK2000™ Temporary Spray Adhesive, Sticky +™ and Tear-Easy™ stabilizers used to make sample.

Cutting

From the batik print:
- Cut one 14 x 42-inch A rectangle.
- Cut three 2¼-inch by fabric width strips for binding.

From the print:
- Cut one 16 x 44-inch B rectangle.

From the batting:
- Cut one 16 x 44-inch rectangle.

Decorative Stitching

1. Draw several 3½-, 5- and 6½-inch circles on the paper side of the self-adhesive fabric stabilizer and cut out on drawn lines.

2. Randomly position circles on right side of rectangle A as desired referring to project photo.

Remove paper backing and adhere circles to right side of rectangle A as positioned.

3. Cut pieces of tear-away fabric stabilizer about 2 inches larger than the circles and spray with temporary adhesive.

4. Position stabilizer under each circle template position on wrong side of A.

5. On the right side of the fabric, using assorted thread weights, colors and stitches, position the presser foot edge along a self-adhesive stabilizer circle edge and slowly sew around curves leaving tails at the beginning and end of stitching. Make sure not to stitch through the stabilizer circles.

6. Peel off circles and reposition them to create overlapping circles.

7. Add concentric rows of stitching by positioning the presser foot edge inside or outside the first stitching line and stitching again referring to photo.

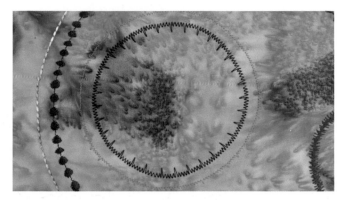

8. Bring all threads to the back and tie off to secure.

9. Supporting the stitches with your fingers, gently tear-away the stabilizer.

Completing the Table Runner

1. When all decorative stitching is complete, mark the center of one short end of A (Figure 1) with a water-soluble marker.

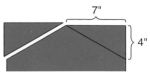

Figure 1

2. Mark 4 inches from the short edge on both long sides referring again to Figure 1. Repeat on opposite end of A.

3. Draw a line connecting the center mark to the side marks. Trim along drawn lines using a rotary cutter to create a pointed end.

4. Lay the pressed backing wrong side up on a flat surface and spray with the temporary fabric adhesive. Smooth the batting into place matching the cut edges.

In-the-Round Challenges

Sewing stitches in a circle can create some challenges, not only as you sew, but at the beginning and end of the stitching.

Stitches are created using a forward motion (scallop stitch) or using a forward and reverse motion (feather stitch).

It's easiest to guide the stitching around a circle if you select stitches that use only a forward motion to create the stitch design.

When using reverse motion stitches, reduce the stitching speed for better control when moving around the circles.

When using bold, contrasting thread colors, alignment problems become more obvious than when sewing with matching thread.

Any discrepancies will show more on solid color background fabrics than prints or tonals.

Even with test stitching, there is really no way to determine the exact alignment of the stitch motifs where the beginning and end of the stitching line meet.

You may have a complete stitch motif aligning perfectly or a partial stitch motif abutting a full motif. It's difficult to get a perfect joining, so just accept that it's part of the technique.

As you complete the circle, you will be able to see how the stitch motifs will align. You can carefully and gently pull the fabric forward or hold it back to join the stitch motifs if the distance between them is minimal.

Always leave long threads at the beginning and end of the stitching line. You can repair partial stitch motifs by hand-stitching using the thread tails.

5. Spray the batting with tempo- rary fabric adhesive and smooth the stitched runner top in place right side up and centered on the backing/batting layers.

6. Join binding strips on short ends with diagonal seams to make one long strip; trim seams to ¼ inch and press seams open (Figure 2).

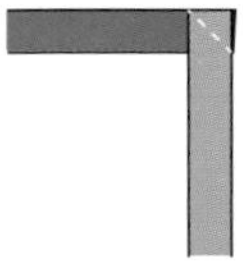

Figure 2

Figure 3

7. Fold the binding strip in half with wrong sides together along length; press. Turn ¼ inch to wrong side at an angle and trim (Figure 3).

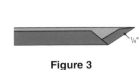

8. Sew binding to right side of table runner stitched top, beginning stitching 1 inch from folded short end, matching raw edges to top and mitering corners.

9. Tuck binding end inside binding beginning and complete stitching.

10. Trim the batting and backing even with the table runner top. Fold the binding to the backing side and hand-stitch the folded edge in place.

11. Hand-stitch a tassel on each end point to complete the table runner. ∎

Wrap It Up

Whether you're expecting a baby or know someone who is, it's easy to make a cozy wrap for the new little bundle of joy. Fleece and flannel team up for snuggly goodness. The fun thing about using decorative stitches on fleece is they sink into the surface and mimic embossing.

Finished Size
40 x 40 inches

Materials
- 1¼ yards 58/60-inch-wide fleece
- 1⅝ yards 45-inch-wide coordinating flannel
- ¾ yard ⅜- to ½-inch-wide narrow lace
- 1-inch-wide ribbon flower
- 30-weight rayon, machine embroidery thread*
- Clear water-soluble stabilizer*
- 4.0mm machine double-needle
- Temporary spray adhesive*
- Walking or even-feed foot (optional)
- Quilting guide (optional)
- Basic sewing supplies and equipment

*Sulky® 30-weight rayon machine embroidery thread, KK2000™ Temporary Spray Adhesive and Solvy™ Stabilizer used to make sample.

Sizing Your Blanket
Baby blankets vary in size with about 30 inches square perfect for a newborn up to crib size, about 48 x 60 inches. Shapes can be square or rectangular, or even a large circle. Consider the fabric width to avoid piecing when you select a size. The featured blanket is 40 inches square.

Cutting

From fleece:
- Cut one 40-inch square.

From flannel:
- Cut five 2½-inch by fabric width binding strips.
- Set aside remainder for blanket backing.

Decorative Stitching
Test-stitch several stitch options on fleece scraps. Some stitches disappear into the fleece fabric surface. Others may be too dense and jam when being stitched causing damage to the fabric.

It is best to work with openwork stitches that sew mostly forward, as opposed to reverse-cycle stitches.

Test stitches on both the length and width of the fleece. Check for distortion and rippling. If rippling occurs, consider using a cut-away stabilizer behind the stitching rows.

1. Select stitches and thread colors.

2. Mark stitching lines 2½, 3¾ and 5 inches from all four sides of the blanket.

Tip
Instead of marking the three stitching lines around the outer edges of the blanket, you can position a piece of painter's tape on the machine bed, 2½ inches from needle, for stitching the first row. Use a quilting guide set for 1¼ inches to stitch two more consecutive rows an equal distance apart.

3. Stitch a row of stitches following each marked line (Figure 1).

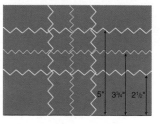

Figure 1

Tip

When you are stitching long rows of decorative stitching, be sure you have lots of thread in the chosen color and a full bobbin.

Check the bobbin periodically to be sure you have enough for the next blanket side to avoid running out in the middle.

Personalizing the Blanket

1. Draw a 3-inch-tall initial inside a 4-inch-diameter circle on a 6-inch square of clear, water-soluble stabilizer.

2. Position and pin the stabilized square on the blanket's right side with the circle's edge 1½ inches from the innermost row of stitching and the monogram at a 45-degree angle to the corner (Figure 2).

Figure 2

3. Using a double-needle, stitch the monogram letter, leaving thread ends long enough to pull to the back and tie off.

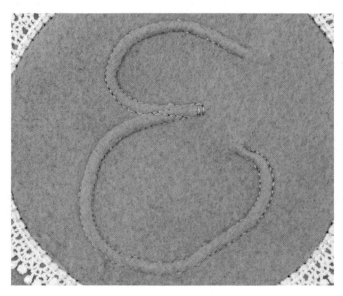

4. Use a single needle to straight-stitch around the circle.

5. Gently tear away the stabilizer while supporting the stitching. Pull threads to wrong side and tie.

6. Position and stitch the narrow lace over the stitched circle line, beginning at the edge closest to the corner and using a narrow appliqué stitch.

7. Sew the ribbon flower where lace ends join.

Assembly

1. Layer and spray-baste fleece blanket wrong sides together with flannel backing. Smooth layers in place, checking for wrinkles on the flannel side.

2. If the fleece distorted during stitching, trim both layers' edges an even distance from the outside stitching lines using a rotary cutter, mat and ruler.

3. Join binding strips on short ends with diagonal seams to make one long strip; trim seams to ¼ inch and press seams open (Figure 3).

Figure 3

4. Fold the binding strip in half with wrong sides together along length; press. Turn ¼ inch to wrong side at a 45-degree angle and trim (Figure 4).

Figure 4

5. Use a walking or even-feed foot to stitch binding to right side of blanket top using a ⅜-inch seam allowance, beginning stitching 1 inch from folded short end, matching raw edges to fleece and mitering corners.

6. Where beginning and end join, tuck binding end inside binding beginning and complete stitching.

7. Fold the binding over the blanket edge to flannel side and hand-stitch in place. ■

Monogram Magic

Audition various type styles in your computer by trying the initial in a number of fonts until you find one you like. The 3-inch letter size is the equivalent of 217 points.

Figure A

Little Black Bag

Basic black silk is a knockout when combined with silver metallic threads for this simple evening bag. Use the chain to make it a shoulder bag, or tuck the chain inside to create a clutch.

Finished Size
7½ x 10 inches

Materials
- ⅝ yard black silk dupioni
- ¼ yard silky print lining
- ⅝ yard lightweight cotton batting*
- ¼ yard lightweight fusible interfacing
- 2 (2-inch) squares of heavyweight interfacing
- 36-inch, small silver chain bag handle set
- 2 (½-inch-diameter) silver jump rings
- ⅝-inch magnetic snap set
- 1-inch-diameter rhinestone button
- Machine needle for metallic thread
- Temporary spray adhesive*
- Metallic embroidery threads*
- Basic sewing supplies and equipment

*Madeira Glamour thread; Coats & Clark metallic embroidery thread; The Warm Company Warm & Natural® batting; Sulky® KK2000™ Temporary Spray Adhesive used to make sample.

Cutting
Use pattern templates for Evening Bag Front/Back and Flap on pages 41 and 42. Transfer all pattern markings to fabric.

From the black silk:
- Cut two 9 x 12-inch rectangles.
- Cut one 7 x 12-inch rectangle.
- Cut one 4½ x 1¼-inch rectangle for chain tabs.
- Cut one bag Flap for lining.

From print lining:
- Cut two Front/Back pieces.

From cotton batting:
- Cut two 9 x 12-inch rectangles.
- Cut one 7 x 12-inch rectangle.

From lightweight fusible interfacing:
- Cut one Flap.

Decorative Stitching
1. Spray-baste the cotton batting 9 x 12-inch rectangles to the wrong sides of the same size black silk rectangles.

2. Quilt the rectangles vertically with rows of wave stitch 1 inch apart referring to Figure 1.

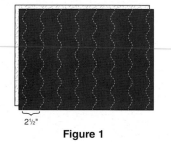

2½"

Figure 1

3. Spray-baste the 7 x 12-inch rectangle cotton batting to the wrong side of the same size black silk rectangle.

4. Use batting and black silk scraps to test and determine metallic threads and decorative stitches.

5. Using chosen assorted metallic threads and decorative stitches, embellish the flap with parallel rows of stitching.

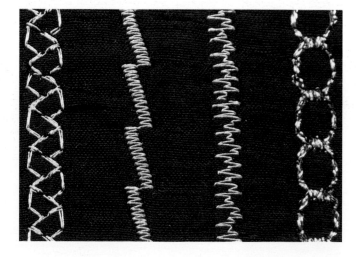

Assembly

Use ¼-inch seam allowances right sides together.

1. Trim quilted 9 x 12-inch and 7 x 12-inch rectangles with bag Front/Back and Flap patterns.

2. Follow manufacturer's instructions to fuse lightweight interfacing Flap to wrong side of black silk Flap lining.

3. Position one heavyweight interfacing square centered over the magnetic snap placement square on wrong side of Flap lining.

4. Following the manufacturer's instructions, apply the magnetic snap fastener male section to the right side of Flap lining at placement square.

5. Apply the female portion of the magnetic snap to the bag front at the snap placement square.

6. To make handle loops, fold and press the 4½ x 1¼-inch rectangle in half lengthwise. Unfold and fold long raw edges to center fold; press. Refold at center and press to make a ⅜-inch-wide strip. Stitch down the center of the strip and cut the strip length in half to make two handle loops.

7. Fold the loop strips in half and baste in place on each side of the bag front lining right side at large circle to form ¾-inch-long loops (Figure 2). Trim excess length if necessary.

Figure 2

Needle Notes

Some metallic threads have a tendency to shred and break as you sew. To help with this, use a needle especially designed for use with metallic threads.

This needle's elongated eye helps reduce abrasion as the thread rides through the needle, helping to reduce breaking and shredding.

These needles are available in sizes 80/12 and 90/14. Match the thread weight to the needle size.

8. Sew the bag front and back lining together matching side notches and leaving a 4-inch opening on bottom edge for turning. Make sure to catch the handle loops in the seam. Do not turn right side out.

9. Stitch the Flap lining to the decorated Flap along the curved edges matching notches. Trim and clip seam (Figure 3). Turn right side out and press edges flat.

Figure 3

10. Match Flap to bag back, matching center notches and small circles; baste in place (Figure 4).

Figure 4

11. Slip the lining over the bag/flap right sides together with flap between bag and lining. Match side seams, pin and stitch around the upper edge.

12. Turn the bag right side out through the lining opening. Tuck lining opening seam allowance to inside and hand- or machine-stitch the opening closed.

13. Press the bag upper edge flat, rolling the lining slightly to the bag inside. Topstitch the bag upper edge.

14. Sew the rhinestone button onto the flap right side centered over the magnetic snap.

15. Use the jump rings to attach the chain handle to the inside handle loops. ■

Metallic Magic

Nothing adds sparkle to a quilted project like metallic accents, and thread manufacturers are quick to offer up many options. Flat foils, some with holographic and pearlescent imaging, offer maximum luminescence. Other options include twisted metallics and those with a fiber-wrapped core.

Metallic threads can be challenging to work with on some machines. To ensure success, try the following:

• Use a vertical spool pin for the thread or a thread stand set to the side of the machine for tangle-free feeding.

• Slow the machine's stitching speed, if possible.

• Select a metallic needle to reduce abrasion.

• Avoid very dense stitch patterning, as metallic threads tend to break if packed tightly.

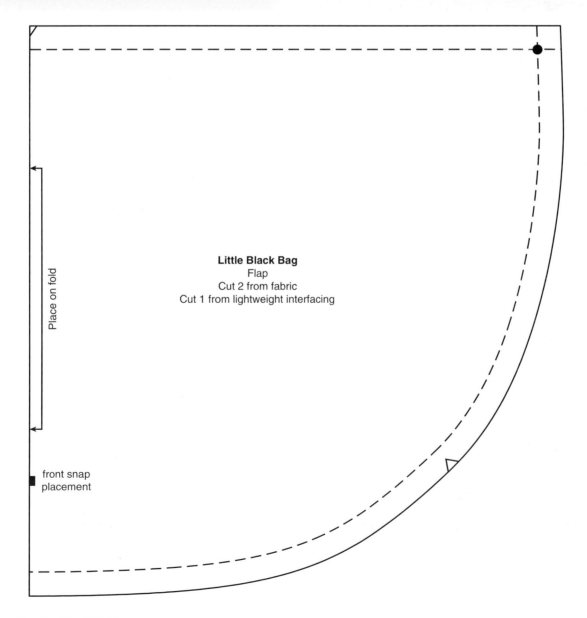

Little Black Bag
Flap
Cut 2 from fabric
Cut 1 from lightweight interfacing

Place on fold

front snap placement

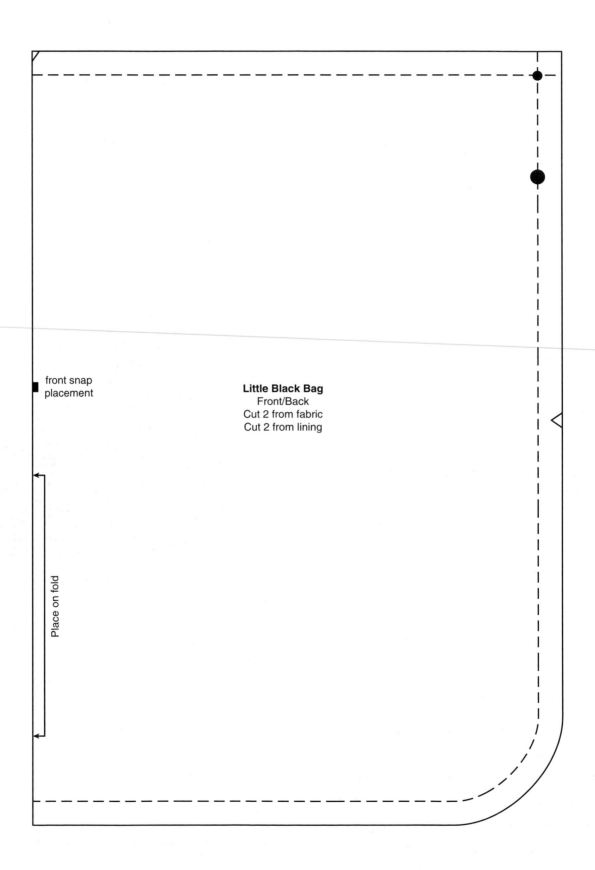

front snap
placement

Little Black Bag
Front/Back
Cut 2 from fabric
Cut 2 from lining

Place on fold

Just Encase Gift-Card Holder

Use decorative stitches to quickly embellish and personalize gift-card boxes. If your machine has wider than normal stitches, the gold band is ideal to showcase them.

Materials

For all versions:

- 1 (12 x 12-inch) sheet of cardstock desired color
- 30-weight rayon, machine embroidery thread*
- Variety Size 5 pearl cotton and/or small yarn
- Tear-away stabilizer*
- Water-soluble stabilizer*
- Bobbin thread to match
- Fabric glue
- Permanent double-sided adhesive tape or paper glue
- Temporary spray adhesive*
- Scoring tool
- Small clips or clothespins
- Basic sewing supplies and equipment

*Beacon Adhesives™ Fabri-Tac™ glue; Sulky® 30-weight rayon machine embroidery thread, KK2000™ Temporary Spray Adhesive, Solvy™ and Tear-Easy™ stabilizers used to make samples.

Box Construction

1. Trace the Gift-Card Holder Box pattern on page 47 onto wrong side of cardstock and cut out.

2. Score firmly along the dashed lines with a scoring tool.

3. Fold the box on the scored lines.

Second Time Around

Once the gift cards have been presented, these stitched trims can have another life. The bands make fun bracelets and the flower is a great ponytail holder. To use as a bracelet, remove all the tear-away stabilizer from the wrong side or back the band with another piece of felt.

4. Apply permanent double-sided adhesive tape or glue to the right side of the flap extension and lap the opposite box edge over the flap. If using glue, clamp in place until dry.

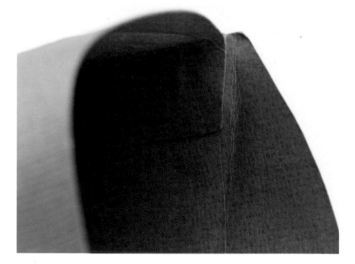

5. Fold box ends over each other.

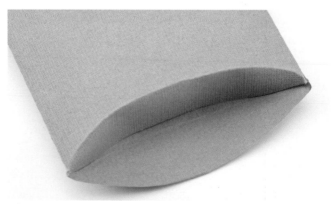

General Band Assembly

1. Apply tear-away stabilizer to the wrong side of the felt with temporary spray adhesive following manufacturer's instructions.

2. Mark a stitching line 1 inch from the right-hand long edge. Measure and mark the desired width of the band to the left of the first line (Figure 1). **Note:** *Samples are 3¼ inches wide.*

Figure 1

3. Choose a decorative stitch and stitch along the first marked line 1 inch from the right-hand edge.

4. Use the mirror-image function on your machine to reverse the decorative stitch direction.

5. Align the left edge of the presser foot with the second drawn line. Stitch a row of reversed decorative stitches along the second marked line, stitching in the same direction as the previous row (Figure 2). **Note:** *If you do not have the mirror-image function, stitch in the opposite direction of the first row of stitching.*

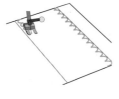

Figure 2

6. Stitch between these two rows of stitching following Decorating Options as desired.

7. Remove the stabilizer along the outside stitching lines. Use small sharp scissors to trim close to the decorative stitching on each edge.

8. Fit the embellished band around the box, overlapping ends. Trim excess length. Overlap ends and stitch together using a straight or narrow zigzag stitch to secure (Figure 3).

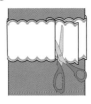

Figure 3

9. Slide the band over the box to complete.

Decorating Options
White Band Assembly
Materials
- 1 (9 x 12-inch) white felt piece
- Tear-away stabilizer
- 30-weight rayon, machine embroidery thread

Assembly
1. Follow steps 1–5 of General Band Assembly on page 43 using white band materials listed, a scallop stitch and 3¼-inch band width.

2. Add two additional stitching rows between the scallops on both sides, leaving space in the center for individual motifs.

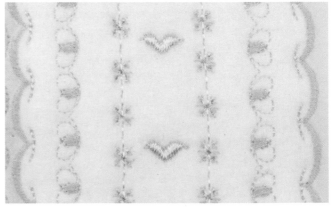

3. Mark individual motif placements in 1-inch increments down the center of the band.

4. Consult your machine manual to set the machine to stitch out single motifs.

5. Stitch individual motifs at each of the 1-inch increments. Clip all thread ends.

6. Follow steps 7–9 of General Band Assembly on page 43 to complete the white band.

Gold Band Assembly

Materials
- 1 (9 x 12-inch) gold felt piece
- Tear-away stabilizer
- 30-weight rayon, machine embroidery thread
- Variety Size 5 pearl cotton and/or small yarn
- Scallop edge scissors or rotary cutter with mat

Assembly

1. Follow steps 1–5 of General Band Assembly on page 43 using gold band materials listed, a decorative stitch of your choice and a 3¼-inch band width.

2. The featured band uses an Omnimotion stitch available on some machines to produce a decorative stitch much wider (up to 60mm wide) than the traditional machine offers. It does this by not only stitching forward, but also side to side. Check to see if your machine offers this stitch option. If not, substitute another stitch built into your machine to create the band borders.

3. Refer to Bobbin Work in the General Instructions on page 10 to stitch center rows of bobbin work.

4. Cut the band edges slightly outside the stitching with scalloped edge scissors or rotary cutter.

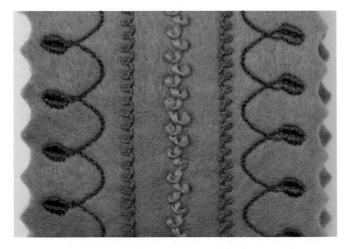

5. Follow steps 8 and 9 of General Band Assembly on page 43 to complete the Gold Band.

Flower Band Assembly

Materials
- 2 x 12-inch strip cotton print fabric
- Size 5 pearl cotton
- Water-soluble stabilizer
- Elastic ponytail fastener
- 1 (1⅜-inch-diameter) button
- Blind hem presser foot

Assembly

1. Fold and press the cotton fabric in half lengthwise.

2. Cut a piece of water-soluble stabilizer the length of the strip. Overlap the stabilizer with the folded fabric edge approximately ½ inch and pin in place (Figure 4).

Figure 4

3. Wind the pearl cotton onto the bobbin and load matching all-purpose thread on your machine for the needle.

4. Attach your blind hem foot to your machine referring to your manual. Set your machine for a blind hemstitch (Figure 5).

5. Stitch the blind hemstitch along the folded edge of the fabric. The zigzag "bite" of the stitch will be on the fabric and the between stitches will be on the water-soluble stabilizer only. Stitch the length of the fold, referring to the photo.

Blind Hemstitch

Figure 5

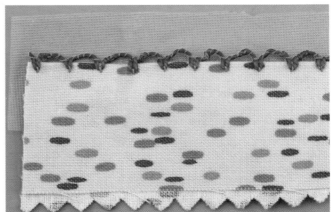

6. Follow the manufacturer's instructions to rinse away the stabilizer. Allow the fabric to dry completely. *Note: For a firmer edge finish, leave some of the water-soluble stabilizer in the fabric—it acts like starch to stiffen the threads.*

7. Sew a basting stitch along the raw edges of the folded fabric strip and pull to gather.

8. Roll the strip into a flower shape, turning under each end at a 45-degree angle. Hand-stitch the rolled strip raw edges together on the wrong side of the flower to hold the shape.

9. Position and stitch the button to the wrong side of the flower.

10. Hand-stitch the flower/button to the ponytail elastic. Slip the elastic around the box to complete. ∎

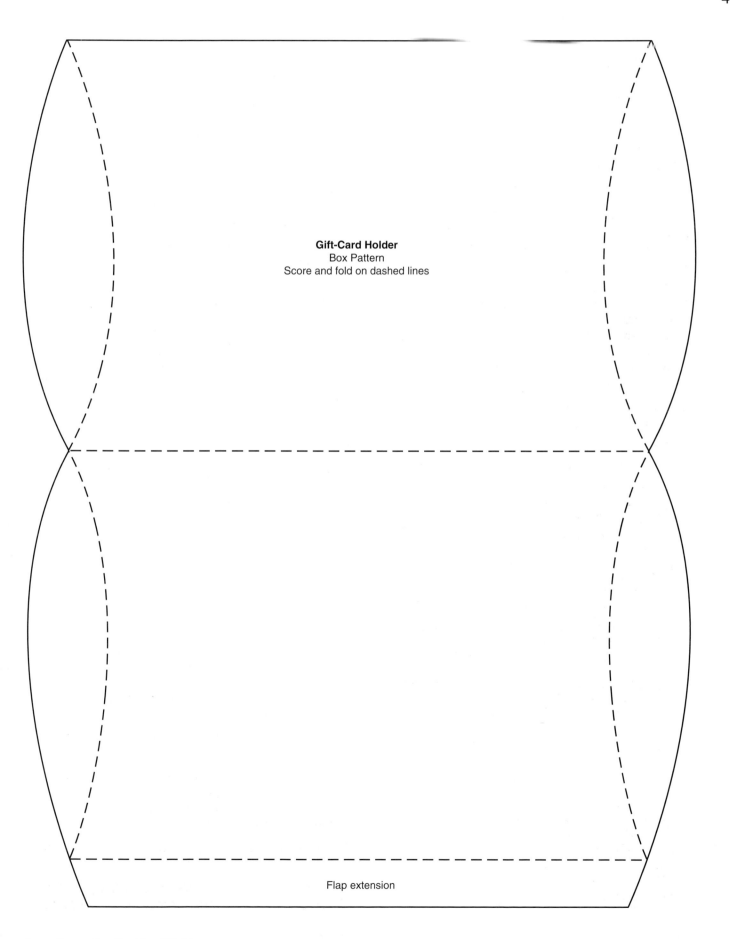

Gift-Card Holder
Box Pattern
Score and fold on dashed lines

Flap extension

Crossing the Line

Showcase decorative stitches on bias tape bands for this fun set of place mats and double-sided napkins. Look for coordinating prints from the same manufacturer, or pick your own combination.

Finished Sizes
Place mat: 13 x 19 inches
Napkin: 18 x 18 inches

Materials
Materials listed make two place mats and napkins each.

- ½ yard large print
- ⅞ yard small coordinating print A
- 1 yard small coordinating print B
- 4 yards single-fold bias tape coordinating solid 1
- 2 yards single-fold bias tape coordinating solid 2
- ½ yard lightweight batting
- ¼- and ½-inch-wide paper-back fusible web tape*
- 30-weight rayon, machine embroidery thread*
- Temporary spray adhesive*
- Walking or even-feed foot (optional)
- Basic sewing supplies and equipment

*The Warm Company Steam-A-Seam 2® paper-back fusible web tape; Sulky® 30-weight rayon machine embroidery thread and KK2000™ Temporary Spray Adhesive used to make samples.

Tip

Bias tape has diagonal seams throughout its length. Purchase a little extra to avoid having to use the seamed areas on your projects. The extra thickness of the seams can cause the machine to distort the stitches slightly over the bulk.

Cutting

From the large print:
- Cut two 13 x 19-inch rectangles.

From coordinating print A:
- Cut two 19-inch squares for napkins.
- Cut four 2¼-inch by width of fabric binding strips.

From coordinating print B:
- Cut two 19-inch squares for napkin lining.
- Cut two 15 x 21-inch rectangles for place mat backings.

From batting:
- Cut two 15 x 21-inch rectangles.

From bias tape solid 1:
- Cut six 20-inch lengths and four 14-inch lengths.

From bias tape solid 2:
- Cut two each 20- and 14-inch lengths.

Place Mats

Decorative Stitching on Bias Bands
1. Follow manufacturer's instructions to apply ½-inch-wide fusible web tape to the wrong side of two each 20- and 14-inch lengths of bias tape solids 1 and 2.

2. Fuse one length of 20-inch solid 1 bias tape centered horizontally 1¾ inches from the lower edge, again following manufacturer's instructions (Figure 1).

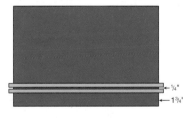

Figure 1

3. Apply a 20-inch solid 2 bias tape length ¼ inch above the first bias length referring again to Figure 1.

4. Prepare samples for test stitching from remnants of fabric and bias tape. Stitching can be placed in the middle of the tape, along one edge, or along both edges, depending on the stitch configuration and the width you select.

5. Select decorative stitches and sew along the bias tape on a place mat rectangle.

6. Repeat steps 1–5 with the vertical bias tape rows. Trim the bias tape edges even with the place mat edges.

Assembly

1. Layer place mat backing wrong side up, and batting and embellished place mat top right side up, centered on batting. Spray-baste layers together, smoothing out any wrinkles.

2. Quilt ½ inch from each bias tape outer edge using the walking or even-feed foot and regular sewing thread.

3. Join binding strips on short ends with diagonal seams to make one long strip; trim seams to ¼ inch and press seams open (Figure 2).

Figure 2

4. Fold the binding strip in half with wrong sides together along length; press. Turn ¼ inch to wrong side at a 45-degree angle and trim (Figure 3).

Figure 3

5. Sew binding to right side of place mat top using a ¼-inch seam, beginning stitching 1 inch from folded short end, matching raw edges to top and mitering corners.

6. Tuck binding end inside binding beginning and complete stitching.

7. Trim the batting and backing even with the place mat top. Fold the binding to the backing side and hand-stitch the folded edge in place.

Napkins

Assembly

1. Prepare, apply and decorate two 20-inch lengths of solid 1 bias tape 2¾ inches from the lower and left side of the coordinating print A napkin referring to Decorative Stitching on Bias Bands on page 49.

2. Stitch decorated napkin top and lining together, using a ½-inch seam and leaving a 3-inch opening on one side for turning. Trim corners at an angle.

3. Turn right side out, gently pushing out corners. Turn opening seam allowance to inside and press edges flat. Hand-stitch opening closed if desired.

4. Topstitch ⅛ inch all around using matching all-purpose thread. ∎

Napkin Note

Napkins can be almost any size you want, from 6-inch cocktail size to 24-inch formal dinner size. The featured napkins are 18 inches square, a perfect dinner size, and they're double-sided so no fabric wrong sides show.

Soft Pocket Lingerie Keeper

Silky satin protects delicate lingerie for traveling. This soft pocket would also make a fun bridal shower gift. Embellish and join assorted laces to decorate the front panel.

Finished Size
10 x 12 inches

Materials
- ¾ yard 44/45-inch-wide polyester satin
- Assorted laces
- ⅓ yard ⅜-inch-wide sheer ribbon (optional)
- 1 yard ¼-inch-wide sheer ribbon
- 1⅛-inch-diameter covered button form
- ¼-inch-wide paper-backed fusible web tape*
- Tear-away stabilizer*
- Temporary spray adhesive*
- Variety 30-weight rayon, machine embroidery threads*
- Basic sewing supplies and equipment

*The Warm Company Steam-A-Seam 2® ¼" fusible web tape; Sulky® 30-weight rayon machine embroidery threads, KK2000™ Temporary Spray Adhesive and Tear-Easy™ stabilizer used to make sample.

Cutting

From polyester satin:
- Cut one 10 x 27-inch rectangle for pocket front panel.
- Cut one 15 x 27-inch rectangle for pocket back.

Decorative Stitches
1. Measure and mark lines 1 inch and 10 inches down from one 10-inch side of the pocket front panel.

> ### Tip
>
> *The yardage of individual laces will vary depending on the width, number of lace pieces and how you join the pieces to embellish the front. You will need at least ⅓ yard of lace for each row spanning the front panel.*

2. Follow manufacturer's instructions to fuse a variety of widths of lace within the marked area with paper-backed fusible web tape (Figure 1).

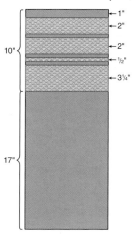

Figure 1

3. Apply tear-away stabilizer to the wrong side of the 10-inch lace area with temporary adhesive.

4. Test assorted stitches on satin and lace scraps backed with stabilizer. Some stitches do not look good when stitched over textured laces.

5. Choose assorted decorative stitches to embellish the laces and hold them in place. Stitching can be done down the lace center or on one or both edges, depending on the desired finished look. Do not remove the stabilizer when stitching is completed.

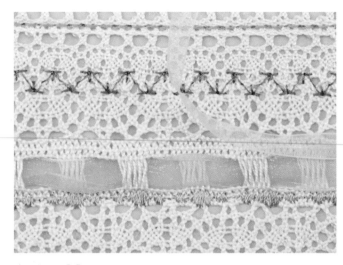

Assembly

Stitch right sides together using a ¼-inch seam allowance unless otherwise indicated.

1. Stitch embellished pocket front panel to pocket back.

2. Press seam allowances open and center the front panel on the back panel, creating a 1¼-inch-wide border on each side. Pin and stitch across the end closest to the lace panel (Figure 2). Turn right side out and press folded edges.

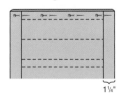

Figure 2

3. With back panel facing up, fold the unstitched end of the satin rectangle in half matching folded edges. Pin and stitch open end together and trim the corners (Figure 3). Press seam open.

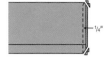

Figure 3

4. Turn stitched end right side out centering the seam on the rectangle width making a pocket flap (Figure 4). Press and pin in place. Hand-stitch the flap folded edge in place.

Figure 4

5. Fold and pin lace end of front panel up 10 inches toward flap to form the pocket shape. Hand-stitch both side edges together along the folds.

6. Fuse a 3-inch section of lace to a scrap of satin and embellish with decorative stitching. Following the manufacturer's instructions, cover the button form with decorated scrap.

7. Sew the button to the flap center 1½ inches above the flap point (Figure 5).

Figure 5

8. Fold the ¼-inch-wide ribbon in half and tack the fold to the lace panel center 2½ inches from the pocket bottom edge (Figure 6).

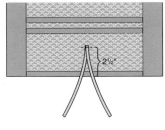

Figure 6

9. Tie the ribbon around the button, trimming extra ribbon length if needed. ◼

It's a Wrap Gift Bag

An eco-friendly and fun way to wrap gifts, this fabric bag can be made in any size to fit the present you need to wrap. The accent band is a great venue for using your decorative stitches—perfect plaids for any occasion.

Finished Size
6 x 12½ inches

Materials
- ⅓ yard red/white dot
- ⅓ yard green plaid lining
- ¼ yard white poplin
- ¾ yard white medium-size rickrack
- 2 yards ½-inch-wide, double-face satin ribbon
- Fusible stabilizer*
- Variety coordinating color 30-weight rayon embroidery threads*
- Quilting guide (optional)
- Basic sewing supplies and equipment

Sulky® 30-weight rayon embroidery threads; Sulky Fuse 'n Stitch™ Iron-on Stabilizer used to make sample.

Cutting

From the red/white dot:
- Cut two 10½ x 13-inch rectangles.
- Cut one 6½-inch-diameter circle.

From the green plaid lining:
- Cut two 10½ x 13-inch rectangles.
- Cut one 6½-inch-diameter circle.

From the white poplin:
- Cut one 7 x 22-inch rectangle.

Decorative Stitches
1. Following the manufacturer's instructions, fuse stabilizer to wrong sides of the white rectangle and the red/white dot circle.

2. Select a decorative stitch and thread colors to use for the plaid patterning. Test-stitch on a stabilized fabric scrap referring to Mad for Plaid on page 56. Make any needed adjustments.

3. Using the first thread color, stitch parallel lines along the rectangle length spaced 1¼ inches apart.

Note: Use a quilting guide for accurate spacing or draw lines with a removable fabric marker on the fabric.

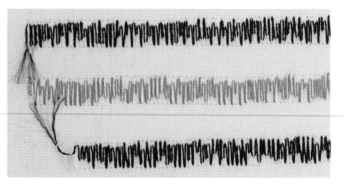

4. Using a second thread color, stitch lines halfway between the previously stitched rows.

5. Using the first thread color, stitch lines 1¼ inch apart perpendicular to the previous rows, and follow with the second thread color centered between the first rows to create the plaid.

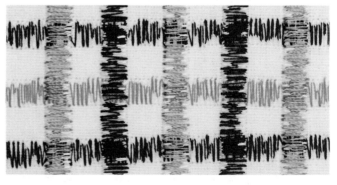

Assembly
Stitch right sides together using a ¼-inch seam allowance unless otherwise indicated.

1. Trim the embellished white rectangle to 6 x 20½ inches, centering the plaid lines along the rectangle height.

2. Position the rickrack along the rectangle right side upper edge and stitch through the center (Figure 1).

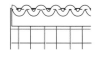

Figure 1

3. Fold upper edge of rectangle to wrong side at seam, pulling rickrack points up above the seam referring to Figure 2.

Figure 2

4. Match 13-inch edges of red/white dot rectangles and stitch one side seam, leaving a 1-inch opening, 2 inches from the upper edge (Figure 3). Press the seam open.

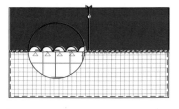

Figure 3

5. Layer the embellished white rectangle right side up onto the bottom of the red/white dot rectangle, matching the lower edges (Figure 4).

Figure 4

6. Stitch in the well of the seam to attach the rickrack edge of the embellished white rectangle to the bag. Baste the remaining raw edges of the embellished white rectangle to the bag referring again to Figure 4.

7. Stitch the remaining side seam in the bag, leaving a 1-inch opening, 2 inches from the upper edge, and matching the rickrack edges of the plaid overlay (Figure 5). Press seam open.

Figure 5

8. Mark the red/white dot circle bottom and the bag bottom edge in quarters.

9. Pin and stitch the bag to the circle bottom, matching the quarter markings. Turn right side out.

10. To make lining, match 13-inch edges of green plaid rectangles and stitch side seams, leaving a 3-inch-long opening in one seam for turning.

11. Attach the circle bottom to the lining following steps 8 and 9. Do not turn lining right side out.

12. Insert the outer bag into the lining, right sides together, matching side seams and top edges.

13. Stitch around the top edge and turn the bag right side out through the lining opening. Press top edge flat. Smooth the lining into place and hand- or machine-stitch the opening closed.

14. To make a drawstring casing, stitch around bag top 1¾ inches and 2¾ inches from top edge (Figure 6).

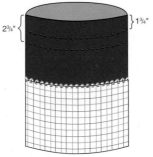

Figure 6

15. Cut the ribbon length in half. Thread one ribbon length through the casing from the right; knot the ends together. Thread second ribbon length

through the casing from the left; knot the ends together (Figure 7). ■

Figure 7

Mad for Plaid

You can make stitched plaids using even an ordinary zigzag stitch. Alter the tension and use a contrasting bobbin thread to create a different look. Test stitches to find an attractive pattern to coordinate with your bag fabric.

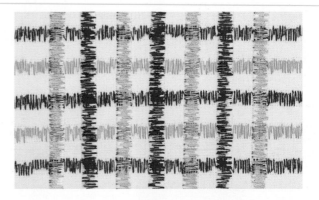

If you prefer to use a border design instead of crisscrossing plaid lines, sew a border using parallel rows of different stitches in a two-color combo.

Middle Management

A perfect way to showcase lots of stitches, this simple-to-sew belt is ideal for trying out new threads and stitches since there's only a short distance to sew for each row. Make it tailored or make it wild!

Finished Size
4 inches wide x your waist size

Materials
- ¼ yard fabric
- ¼ yard lining
- ¼ yard 45-inch-wide heavyweight fusible interfacing
- 2 yards ¼-inch-wide cord or flat braid
- 2 (⅜-inch) grommets
- Fusible stabilizer*
- Variety 30-weight rayon embroidery threads*
- Tailor's chalk
- Basic sewing supplies and equipment

*Sulky® 30-weight rayon machine embroidery threads; Sulky Fuse 'n Stitch™ Iron-on Stabilizer used to make sample.

Sizing Your Belt
To determine the belt length, comfortably measure your waistline and use this measurement as the cut length. Alter the belt width as desired.

The amount of 44/45-inch-wide fabric listed in the materials list will accommodate belt lengths up to 40 inches.

Decorative Stitches
1. Follow the manufacturer's instructions to apply heavyweight fusible interfacing to the wrong side of the fabric yardage.

2. Apply stabilizer to the wrong side of the interfaced fabric following the manufacturer's instructions.

Tip

If your waistline isn't something you want to accent, use this same technique on a purse handle, bell pull, or make the strip wider and make a table runner.

3. Draw the belt shape onto the right side of the fabric rectangle with tailor's chalk, using determined length, desired width and rounding ends.

4. Choose decorative stitches and threads desired. Randomly draw stitching lines or do a free-form stitch pattern.

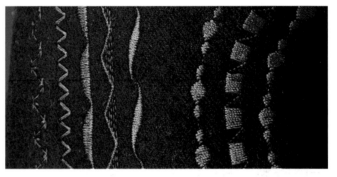

5. Stitch rows in desired pattern onto the rectangle, extending the stitching rows slightly past the drawn belt shape lines.

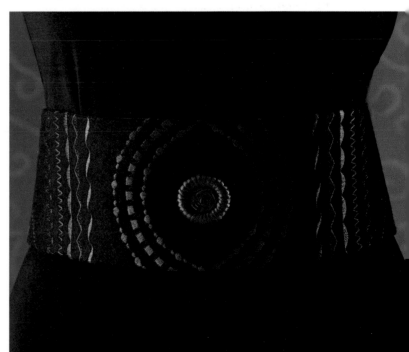

6. If you would like to make a reversible belt, embellish the lining fabric following steps 1–5.

Assembly

Stitch right sides together using a ¼-inch seam allowance unless otherwise indicated.

1. Trim the belt and lining on the drawn lines. ***Note:*** *If you did not embellish the lining, use the belt as a pattern and cut out a lining to match.*

2. Stitch the lining to the belt, leaving a 3-inch opening for turning on one long side (Figure 1).

Figure 1

Piping With Purpose

To create a decorative piping, begin with ready-made piping from the trim department.

Install the buttonhole or cording foot on the machine so the piping cord can ride underneath it during stitching.

Select a stitch that will go over the piping cord and embellish the length needed for your project.

3. Trim seams, clip curves and turn the belt right side out.

Tip

For quicker curve trimming and clipping at one time, use pinking shears that cut little notches into the seam allowances.

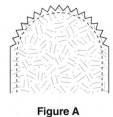

Figure A

4. Hand-stitch the opening closed. Press the edges flat.

5. Following the manufacturer's instructions, apply grommets 1 inch from the curved belt ends and centered on the belt width (Figure 2).

Figure 2

6. Cut the cord length in half and thread each half through the one grommet (Figure 3). Knot or sear cord ends to prevent raveling.

Figure 3

7. Use the same tie for both sides on a reversible belt, or switch out the ties when you turn the belt over. ■

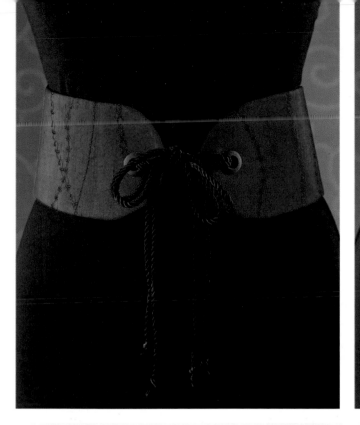

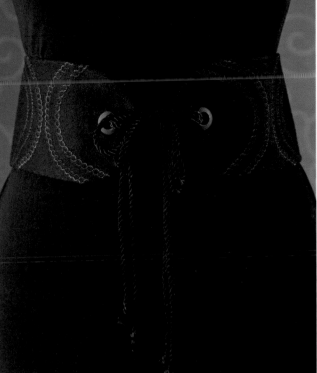

Beyond the Basics

This belt design offers a lot of room for embellishment options, depending on the fabric and the stitches you choose. Use any of the techniques presented in this book to decorate it.

To change up the belt, try one or more of these options:

- Tie the belt in the front or in the back. If you choose to tie it in the back, add a decoratively shaped pattern at the belt center to create a focal point and perhaps add a button, pin or medallion.

- Accent the stitching lines with beads, buttons or sequins for a dressier look.

- Use plaid or stripe fabric and follow the lines with decorative stitching.

- Add lightweight batting for a quilted look.

- Use faux leather or faux suede and stitch openwork stitching lines. Remember: Dense designs can damage these fabrics.

- Reshape the end of the belt.

- Embellish piping with decorative stitches and sew it into the outer belt seam referring to Piping With Purpose on page 58.

- Use the straight stretch stitch (two stitches forward, one back) with novelty threads for a prominent stitch.

- Stitch lines asymmetrically for a whimsical look.

Yipes, Stripes! Tote

You can never have too many totes. And this one, with juxtaposed stripes, is a great canvas for showcasing your machine's stitches. Look in the decorator section of the fabric store for sturdy stripes for all seasons and simply follow the lines to stitch.

Finished Size
4 x 14 x 16 inches

Materials
- 1¼ yards narrow striped cotton duck-weight fabric
- ⅝ yard lining fabric
- All-purpose thread
- 1¼ yards medium-weight fusible interfacing
- 1⅓ yards 1-inch-wide cotton webbing
- 4 x 14-inch rectangle plastic canvas
- 30-weight rayon, machine embroidery thread*
- Cut-away or tear-away stabilizer*
- Temporary spray adhesive*
- Basic sewing supplies and equipment

Sulky® 30-weight rayon machine embroidery thread, Tear-Easy™ stabilizer and KK2000™ Temporary Spray Adhesive used to make sample.

Cutting
From the stripe fabric:
- Cut one each 10½ x 11½-inch lower bag and 10½ x 9-inch upper bag rectangles on the crosswise grain and one each on the lengthwise grain referring to the cutting diagram.
- Cut one 20 x 19½-inch bag back rectangle by folding remaining fabric in half along lengthwise grain and cutting one 10 x 19½-inch rectangle along fold referring again to cutting diagram.

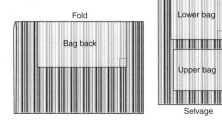

Cutting Diagram

From medium-weight fusible interfacing:
- Cut two each 10½ x 11½-inch lower bag and 10 x 11½-inch upper bag rectangles and one 20 x 20-inch square for bag back.

From lining:
- Cut two 17½ x 20-inch rectangles for lining.

From webbing:
- Cut two 24-inch lengths for bag straps.

Decorative Stitching
1. Follow the manufacturer's instructions and fuse the interfacing to the corresponding bag pieces.

2. Spray the wrong sides of the front bag pieces with temporary adhesive and apply stabilizer.

3. Follow the stripe lines on the front bag pieces to embellish the pieces with various decorative stitches referring to Stripe to It on page 63.

Tip
Work on all four bag front pieces at once to sew common stitches and thread colors. It saves repeatedly changing threads and resetting stitches. Simply vary the location of the same stitch if you repeat it.

4. Remove the stabilizer from the seam allowances—the rest of it can stay put.

Assembly
Use ½-inch seam allowances. Interfacing does not appear in drawings.

1. Fold bag back and bag lining pieces in half, lengthwise right sides together. Mark and cut a

2 x 1½-inch rectangle out of the bottom left-hand corner opposite the fold from both pieces (Figure 1).

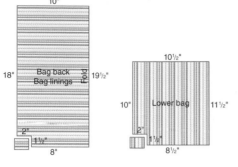

Figure 1

2. Layer lower bag rectangles right sides together. Mark and cut a 2 x 1½-inch rectangle out of the lower left-hand corner of the 11½-inch side referring again to Figure 1.

3. Sew the uncut 11½-inch sides of the lower bag pieces together referring to Figure 2. Press seam allowance to one side.

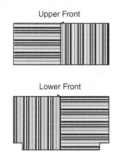

Figure 2

4. Stitch upper bag pieces together along 9-inch sides referring again to Figure 2. Press seam allowance in opposite direction of lower bag. *Note: Make sure the stripes go in opposite directions between the upper and lower bag pieces.*

5. Sew the upper and lower bag sections together matching the center seams.

6. Sew the pieced bag front to the bag back at the side and lower edges; press the seams open (Figure 3).

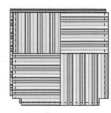

Figure 3

7. Fold the bag corner edges together matching side and bottom seams and stitch to box the corners (Figure 4).

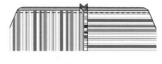

Figure 4

8. Turn the bag right side out and press the upper edge 1½ inches to wrong side to make top hem allowance.

9. Unfold the hem and position the webbing handles centered at the upper edge 5 inches apart (Figure 5).

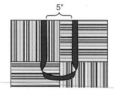

Figure 5

10. Stitch a box with an X in the middle on each handle end within the hem area referring to Figure 6.

Figure 6

11. Stitch bag lining side and bottom seams together leaving a 4-inch opening for turning in the bottom seam. Box the corners referring to step 7.

12. Insert bag into lining right sides together with handles between and matching top edges. Stitch together.

13. Turn bag right side out through lining opening. Push lining into bag and press lining away from top hem allowance.

14. Stitch-in-the-ditch of the side and center front seams to hold the hem in place.

15. Hand-stitch bottom lining opening together.

16. Cut a 9 x 15-inch rectangle from the striped scraps. Stitch together along long side and one short end. Clip corners at an angle. Turn right side out; gently push out corners.

17. Insert plastic canvas rectangle into stitched striped rectangle. Turn open end to inside and hand-stitch closed.

18. Hand-stitch covered plastic canvas rectangle to the tote lining bottom catching the ends at the corner seams to hold it in place. ▪

Stripe to It

Working with stripes makes embellishing with decorative stitches easier than ever—there are no lines to draw for placement, no guides to follow—just follow the stripes.

Center stitches down a stripe or use the stitches to border a stripe. Doing both can make a stripe look like a ribbon trim.

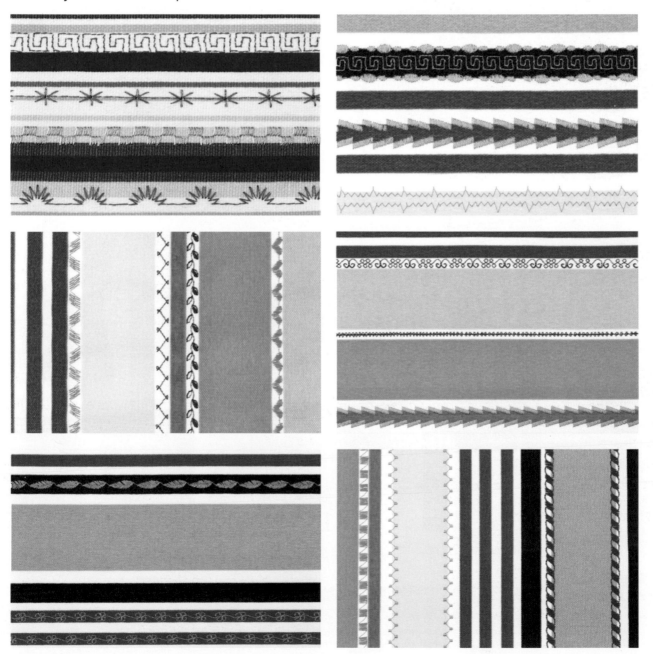

Sources

Projects within this book each have a listing of specific products used in making them. For more information on these products and how to purchase them, visit the company websites listed below.

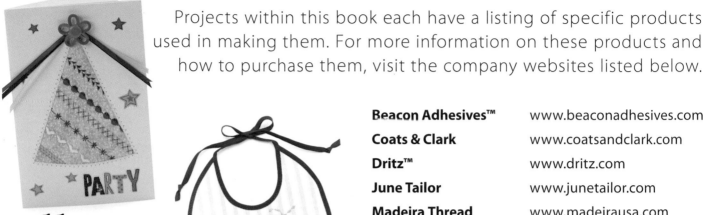

11

17

Beacon Adhesives™	www.beaconadhesives.com
Coats & Clark	www.coatsandclark.com
Dritz™	www.dritz.com
June Tailor	www.junetailor.com
Madeira Thread	www.madeirausa.com
Paper Creations	www.papercreations.com
Sulky of America	www.sulky.com
The Warm Company	www.warmcompany.com

Photo Index

20 **24** **28** **31** **34** **38**

43 **49** **51** **54** **57** **60**

Learn Decorative Machine Stitching is published by Annie's, 306 East Parr Road, Berne, IN 46711. Printed in USA. Copyright © 2013 Annie's. All rights reserved. This publication may not be reproduced in part or in whole without written permission from the publisher.

RETAIL STORES: If you would like to carry this pattern book or any other Annie's publications, visit AnniesWSL.com.

Every effort has been made to ensure that the instructions in this pattern book are complete and accurate. We cannot, however, take responsibility for human error, typographical mistakes or variations in individual work. Please visit AnniesCustomerCare.com to check for pattern updates.

ISBN: 978-1-59217-486-7
1 2 3 4 5 6 7 8 9